Martial Arts Culture of Foshan China

中国佛山功夫文化

佛山历史文化丛书·功夫

张雪莲 著　王立国 改编
许勉君 译

广州新华出版发行集团
广州出版社

图书在版编目（CIP）数据

中国佛山功夫文化 / 张雪莲著；王立国改编；许勉君译. —广州：广州出版社，2020.10
（佛山历史文化丛书）
ISBN 978-7-5462-3098-6

Ⅰ.①中… Ⅱ.①张… ②王… ③许… Ⅲ.①武术—文化—佛山—汉、英 Ⅳ.①G852

中国版本图书馆CIP数据核字（2020）第149456号

书　　名 中国佛山功夫文化
Zhongguo Foshan Gongfu Wenhua
出版发行 广州出版社
（地址：广州市天河区天润路87号9楼、10楼　邮政编码：510635
网址：www.gzcbs.com.cn）
出 版 人 柳宗慧
策　　划 佛山日报社
责任编辑 蚁燕娟　叶桂莲　刘雅丽
责任校对 李少芳
责任技编 刘雁明
装帧设计 紫上视觉 刁俊锋+黄隽琳
题　　字 庞国钟
插　　画 王淼冰
印刷单位 广州市赢彩彩印有限公司
（地址：广州市白云区嘉禾鹤边鹤泰东路工业区C栋自编6号　邮政编码：511440）
规　　格 889毫米×1194毫米　1/32
字　　数 200千
印　　张 8.5
版　　次 2020年10月第1版
印　　次 2020年10月第1次
书　　号 ISBN 978-7-5462-3098-6
定　　价 68.00元

“佛山历史文化丛书”
编辑委员会

Foshan History and Culture Series Editorial Board

目　录

CONTENTS

中国佛山功夫文化

Martial Arts Culture of Foshan China

FOSHAN, CHINA

第一章

佛山武术历史溯源

Chapter 1

Origin of Foshan Martial Arts

2004年，中国广东省佛山市被中国国家体育总局授予“武术之城”称号。佛山武术历史悠久，具有广泛的群众基础和深厚的文化底蕴。它的孕育、发展和传播，与这一地域的自然环境、人文环境息息相关，为各种内外因素交替影响过程中产生的非物质文化遗产。

In 2004, Foshan was entitled "City of Martial Arts" by the General Administration of Sport of China. Foshan martial arts are time-honored, popular and culturally rooted. Closely related to the natural and human environments, they are an intangible cultural heritage produced by the various internal and external factors.

1.1 Foshan Regional Environment and City Construction

Foshan, located in the northwest of the Pearl River Delta Plain in central Guangdong, is at the juncture of East and Southeast Asia, whose economy develops vigorously. It reaches the Foshan Creek in the east, and the Dongping River in the south. Its terrain slopes from the northwest to the southeast. Surrounded by water, Foshan is an important pass to Guangzhou from the Xijiang River and the Beijiang River. Lying at the intersection of two economic development axes, namely, the west-east Zhaoqing-Foshan-Guangzhou-Huizhou and the north-south Guangzhou-Foshan-Zhuhai-Macao, it is a gateway and link to the western mountainous areas and the southwest of Guangdong.

Foshan has a mild subtropical monsoon climate, abundant rainfall and spring-like seasons. With the Xijiang and Beijiang rivers and their tributaries in the Pearl River Water System running through the city, it has a typical delta river network. It is a famous water city with an advantageous geographical location, numerous talents, and prosperous traditional handicrafts, industry and commerce.

Before the Yuan Dynasty (1271-1368), Foshan had no grass-root administrative construction and belonged to Nanhai County, Guangzhou Prefecture. *Nanhai Chronicle* in the Dade period of the Yuan Dynasty only had the words "Foshan Du (ferry)" about Foshan. At the end of the Yuan Dynasty, the title "Jihua Xiang (village)" appeared.

During the Hongwu period of the Ming Dynasty (1368-1644), Foshan was first called "Foshan Bu, Xilin Du, Wudoukou Division, Nanhai County, Guangzhou Prefecture. At that time, there were 64 Bu in six Du in Nanhai County and Foshan was one of the 10 Bu of Xilin Du. In the meantime, Foshan was also called Jihua Xiang which was one of the seven townships of Nanhai County".

第一节 佛山区域环境和城市建置

佛山地处亚太经济发展活跃的东亚与东南亚交汇处，位于广东省中部珠江三角洲平原西北部，东以佛山涌为界，南部以东平河为界，地势自西北向东南倾斜。佛山四面环水，地扼西江和北江干流通往广州的要冲。处于东西向的肇—佛—穗—惠与南北向的穗—佛—珠—澳两条经济发展轴线的交会点上，为通向粤西广大山区以及粤西南地区的门户和纽带。

佛山气候温和、雨量充沛、四季如春，属亚热带季风气候。珠江水系中的西江、北江（及其支流）贯穿全境，属典型的三角洲河网地区，为珠江三角洲的泽国水乡。优越的地理位置，促使人文荟萃，传统手工业和工商经济十分繁荣。

元以前，佛山并无基层行政建置，属于广州府南海县。元大德《南海志》关于佛山的记载仅有“佛山渡”三个字。元末，开始出现“季华乡”的称谓。

明洪武年间，佛山始称“广州府南海县五斗口司西淋都佛山堡，当时南海县有六都六十四堡，佛山为西淋都十堡之一。同时，佛山又称为季华乡，南海县当时有七乡，季华乡属其中之一”[1]。在佛山，季华

1 清康熙《南海县志》。

乡的地理概念与佛山堡是一致的。此时，宗族势力引起的社会矛盾激化，为佛山武术的形成提供了条件。

明中叶至清代，佛山的手工业和工商业进入隆盛时期，成为“粤一大都会”。佛山与江西景德镇、河南朱仙镇、湖北汉口镇并称为中国“四大名镇”。

民国时期，佛山为南海一镇，人口已经超过了30万人。

1924年，佛山第一次设立市政体制，直隶广东省，设立市政厅。

1934年，佛山市改为南海县特别区。

1949年10月，重新设立佛山市。

1950年7月，改市为镇。

1951年6月，改镇为市，辖区主要为原佛山镇。至此，佛山市行政范围大体上是原佛山镇范围。

1954年，石湾划归佛山市管辖。

1956年，设立佛山专区，辖佛山、江门、石岐3个市和中山等13个县。

1970年，佛山专区更名为佛山地区，辖14个县（市）。

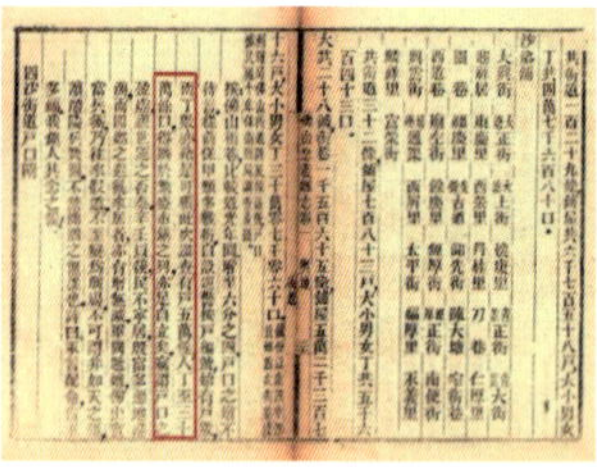

民国乡志记载的佛山人口

Foshan population recorded in township chronicle of the Republic of China

1983年6月，开始实行市领县的体制，辖城区、石湾区两区和中山、南海、顺德、高明、三水等5个县。

2002年12月，城区、石湾区和南海市南庄镇整合成佛山市禅城区，南海、顺德、三水、高明撤市设区，形成佛山辖5个区的格局。

The geographical concepts of Foshan Bu and Jihua Xiang were the same[1]. At that time, the intensifying social conflicts between different clans prepared for the formation of martial arts in Foshan.

From the mid-Ming Dynasty to the Qing Dynasty, handicrafts, industry and commerce of Foshan were blooming, turning it into a metropolis in Guangdong. Foshan, Jingdezhen in Jiangxi, Zhuxianzhen in Henan, and Hankou in Hubei were collectively called the "Four Famous Towns" in China.

During the period of the Republic of China (1912-1949), Foshan was a town of Nanhai County, with a population of over 300,000.

In 1924, Foshan first established its city-level administration and its city hall, which was under the direct jurisdiction of Guangdong Province.

In 1934, Foshan City was renamed Special Zone of Nanhai County.

In October 1949, Foshan City was re-established.

In July 1950, the city was changed into a town.

In June 1951, Foshan Town was changed into Foshan City, governing over the original Foshan Town. By then, the administrative range of Foshan City was basically the same as that of Foshan Town.

In 1954, Shiwan was placed under the jurisdiction of Foshan City.

In 1956, Foshan Special Zone was established, governing over the three cities of Foshan, Jiangmen and Shiqi and 13 counties including Zhongshan.

In 1970, Foshan Special Zone was renamed Foshan District, governing over 14 counties (and cities).

From June 1983, the system of city governing counties was initiated, so Foshan governed Urban District, Shiwan District and five counties including Zhongshan, Nanhai, Shunde, Gaoming and Sanshui.

In December 2002, the original Urban District, Shiwan District and Nanzhuang Town of Nanhai City were integrated into Chancheng District of Foshan City, and Nanhai, Shunde, Sanshui and Gaoming became districts of Foshan, thus forming the pattern of one city governing five districts.

---

1 *Naihai County Chronicle* of the Kangxi period.

1.2 A Long History of Foshan Martial Arts

More than 5,000 years ago, in the center of the Pearl River Delta gathered a tribe of the ancient Yue ethnic group, who mainly lived on fishing and hunting, and some mountain-collecting economy. They were good at making pottery with geometric patterns, bone artifacts, jade and other handicrafts. In their survival and struggle against nature, the pioneers created tools such as stone knives, stone chisels, stone cones, bone forks, bone cones and bone arrows.

Scholars maintain that the use of such tools embodies the wisdom of the primitive people. In the process of weapon confrontation and freehand fighting, they had formed the skills of punching, kicking, flexing, and using weapons, all of which bred the birth of martial arts.

During the Spring and Autumn period and the Warring States period (B.C.770-B.C.221), Guangxi and Guangdong were the habitats of the two branches of Baiyue ethnic group called Xi'ou and Luoyue. At that time, martial arts were developed to a certain level and popularized in society

Archaeological findings show that in the Western Han Dynasty, there were already sword-bearers in Foshan. With the appearance and widespread use of

澜石后冈出土的西汉墓葬铜剑（佛山市博物馆藏）

A bronze sword unearthed from a Western Han tomb at Hougang, Lanshi (stored in Foshan Museum)

第二节 佛山武术源远流长

5000多年前，珠三角中心区一个以捕鱼、狩猎为主，兼有山冈采集经济，擅长制作几何印文陶器、骨器、玉石等手工制品的古越族先民部落在这里繁衍生息。先人们在生存及与自然的斗争中，创造出石刀、石凿、石锥、骨叉、骨锥和骨箭镞等工具。

学者认为，这些工具的使用，体现了原始先民的智慧。在器械交锋和徒手搏击的过程中，逐步形成了拳打脚踢、闪展腾挪和使用器械的技能，武术孕育渐露曙光。

春秋战国时期，两广地区为西瓯和骆越两个百越族支系的生息地，武术已具一定水平，并在社会中相当普及。

据考古发现，西汉时期佛山已有佩剑之人。当时随着刀的出现及在战场上的广泛使用，剑逐渐退出了战场，但在民间得到更大的发展[1]。东汉时期，佛山人已掌握先进的耕作技术，佛山成为鱼米之乡。

唐宋时期，中国武术迅速发展，并逐步走向成熟。随着宋人南迁，中原武术与百越武术得以交融发展。佛山从一个渔村圩市逐渐

1 南海市地方志编辑委员会：《南海县志》，中华书局2000年版，第1156页。

变成一个初兴的手工业、工商业城镇。

1841年佛山铸造的五千斤铁炮
The 2,500-kilogram iron cannon forged in Foshan in 1841

明清时期，佛山的海外贸易日渐繁荣，经济发展更快，冶铁、制陶、纺织、中成药等手工业和产业经济已相当发达。除了铁镬等日用器具、农具和铁钟、佛像等艺术精品，各种制式的铁炮、大铳、流弹等兵器，包括东莞虎门清代大炮、佛山市祖庙博物馆“褒宠”牌坊前的清代铁炮等都是佛山的产品。

武器生产为军事对抗和势力抗争提供了支持，而使用这些武器的人需要长期的训练与技术的支撑，这从侧面反映了佛山拥有使用这些武器的人才。

knives in battle fields, swords gradually withdrew from military use but were further developed among the civilians [1]. In the Eastern Han Dynasty, Foshan people already knew advanced farming techniques, turning the place into a land of fish and rice.

During the Tang and Song dynasties, Chinese martial arts developed rapidly and matured gradually. As the Song people moved south, martial arts of the Central Plain and of Baiyue developed in harmony. Foshan was gradually transformed from a fishing village into an emerging town of handicrafts, industry and commerce.

During the Ming and Qing dynasties, Foshan witnessed prosperity of overseas trade and more rapid economic development. Handicrafts and industries of iron smelting, ceramics, textiles and patent TCM (traditional Chinese medicine) were well developed. Apart from daily utensils such as iron wok, agricultural tools, and artifacts such as iron bells and Buddha statues, iron cannons, blunder-busses, stray bullets, and other weapons, including the Qing Dynasty cannon in Humen, Dongguan, and the iron cannon in front of the "Baochong" Memorial Gateway in Foshan Ancestral Temple Museum, were all products of Foshan.

Weapon production provided support for armed confrontation and power struggle, while people using these weapons had to rely on long-term training and technical support, which indirectly reflects that Foshan had talents to use these weapons.

1 The Editorial Committee of Nanhai City Chronicles. *Nanhai Country Chronicle.* Beijing: Zhonghua Book Company, 2000, p.1156.

1.3 Huang Xiaoyang Rebellion Prompting Establishment of Local Armed Forces

In the 14th year of the Zhengtong period (1449) of the Ming Dynasty, Huang Xiaoyang (originally named Huang Maosong) of Pancun Village, Chonghe Bu, Nanhai County attacked Foshan with tens of thousands of rioters, resulting in the most serious social unrest in Guangdong in the Ming Dynasty.

The seniors and the brave people of Foshan, led by the head of the township Xian Haotong, organized self-defense battles with locally made weapons for a fortnight, killing thousands of invaders until Huang Xiaoyang retreated. This event had far-reaching influences, revealing the fact that both armies had talent excellent in strategy and brave in fighting; and that close combats required a strong physique, long-term training and clever use of martial arts. Later, the imperial court cracked down on the rebellious force and Huang was defeated.

清代佛山民间使用的武器（佛山市博物馆藏）

Weapons used by Foshan folks in the Qing Dynasty (stored in Foshan Museum)

In the first year of the Jingtai period (1450) of the Ming Dynasty, Foshan was awarded by the emperor as the "Town of Loyalty and Righteousness". The elders of Foshan, as conscientious defenders of peace and security of their hometown, led the local people

第三节　黄萧养起事促进地方武装建立

明正统十四年（1449），南海县冲鹤堡潘村黄萧养（原名黄懋松）聚数万之众攻打佛山，造成明代广东地区最严重的一次社会动荡。

佛山耆老乡勇以乡长冼灏通为首，组织自卫，运用本地打制的武器，开展有组织的防守战事，坚守半月，杀敌数千，直至黄萧养退兵。这场战事可谓影响深远，同时体现了两军阵营中精于谋略、骁勇善战者大有人在——近身肉搏之人，必须具备强健的体格，有长期训练的基础，运用智慧以求获胜。

之后朝廷派军镇压，黄军败。

明景泰元年（1450）佛山被敕封为“忠义乡”。

明嘉靖四年（1525）立“忠义鸿名重地”木匾

Wooden plague of “Important Place of Loyalty and Righteousness” erected in the fourth year of Jiajing Period (1525) of the Ming Dynasty

佛山耆老作为家乡安定的自觉维护者，率领子弟乡勇，手拿棍棒锄头，英勇奋战。他们能有如此作为，除了凭借忠义之气外，离不开长期有效的技术训练和当地武术的普及与繁荣。

to fight bravely with clubs and hoes. Apart from their spirit of loyalty and righteousness, their heroic deeds were inseparable from their long-term and effective skill training and the popularization and prosperity of martial arts.

1.4 From Loyalty and Righteousness Camp to Four Government Offices

In the 42nd year of the Wanli period (1614) of the Ming Dynasty, in accordance with the mandate of the imperial court, Li Daiwen, a *Jinshi* (a successful candidate in the highest imperial examinations) from Foshan established the Loyalty and Righteousness Camp, the earliest armed institution for organized local autonomy in Foshan.

In the fourth year of the Shunzhi period (1647) of the Qing Dynasty, *Tongpan* (a prefecture-level official) Tu Biao was stationed in Foshan to maintain social public security so that the place started to have a stationed army.

In the seventh year of the Shunzhi period (1650), *Tongzhi* (a deputy head of a prefecture) Guan Yu went to Foshan and made his garrison office at the back street of Yaqian (now Dongfang Square, Chancheng District).

In the third year of the Kangxi period (1664) of the Qing Dynasty, Foshan practiced the *Baojia* system (a grass-root administrative system), under which there was a head of each Bao, and the households were numbered. In the same year, Feng Shikui, a touring inspector of Wudoukou Division was transferred from Pingzhou, Nanhai in Guangzhou Prefecture to Shanzipu in Foshan. His office was established at Yapang Street.

In the 11th year of the Yongzheng period (1733) of the Qing Dynasty, the Branch Government Office of Foshan, Nanhai County, Guangzhou Prefecture was established, which was later moved to Xiuyan Fu Academy (now in Foshan No.3 Middle School on Weiguo Road).

The Office of the *Qianzong* (a low-ranking military official) was headquartered at Caiyangtang Boulevard. The above-mentioned garrison office, the inspector's

第四节 从忠义营到文武四衙

明万历四十二年（1614），进士出身的佛山人李待问遵朝廷制创设的忠义营，为佛山最早有组织的地方自治武装机构。

清顺治四年（1647），通判屠彪到佛山驻防，维护社会治安，佛山始有驻防军队。

清顺治七年（1650），同知官玉到佛山，驻防官署设在衙前后街（今禅城区东方广场位置）。

清康熙三年（1664），佛山镇施行保甲制，设保长，编门牌。同年，五斗口司巡检冯士魁由广州府南海平洲迁驻佛山山紫铺。都司衙门设在衙旁街。

清雍正十一年（1733）设置广州府南海县佛山分府衙门，府衙后来迁往秀岩傅公祠（今卫国路佛山市第三中学校内）。

千总衙门设在彩阳堂大街。上述驻防官署、都司衙门、佛山分府衙门、千总衙门共称文武四衙。

官府对于佛山的军事控制在清咸丰四年（1854）后明显加强，谢效庄为督捕首领，水陆两路分兵镇守。

office, the branch government office and the *Qianzong* office were collectively called the four administrative and military offices.

Since the fourth year of the Xianfeng period (1854) of the Qing Dynasty, the imperial government markedly strengthened its military control over Foshan, manifested by the fact that Xie Xiaozhuang led the arrest supervision division to guard the city with both water and land troops.

1.5 Imperial Martial Examinations in the Ming and Qing Dynasties in Foshan

In history, five Marital Champions in imperial martial examinations were from Guangdong Province, including Zhu Kezhen, Lin Deyong, Li Weiguang, Huang Renyong and Yao Daning, among whom Zhu Kezhen was from Shunde, Foshan and Yao Daning from Nanhai, Foshan.

I. Zhu Kezhen, the Martial Champion in the Ming Dynasty

Zhu Kezhen (years of birth and death unknown) was a native of Longjiang, Shunde. With his powerful arms, he was able to bend a strong bow and hit the target without a single miss. Additionally, he was capable of wielding a broadsword superbly.

In the fourth year of the Tianqi period (1624), Zhu went to the capital Beijing for the metropolitan examination and successfully became a metropolitan graduate, qualifying for the palace examination. In the palace examination, he became the champion. Therefore, he was first appointed as Assistant Regimental Commander in the Imperial Guards, and then designated as Associate Central Military Chief, and conferred the title of General Zhao. Due to his impartiality, Zhu was once transferred to crack down on pirates in Guangdong Province.

II. Yao Daning, Martial Champion in the Qing Dynasty

Yao Daning (1772-1807) was from Wenjiao Village, Heshun Town, Nanhai.

Yao sat for the imperial martial examination in the fourth year of the Jiaqing

第五节　明清时期佛山武科

历史上，广东共有朱可贞、林德镛、李威光、黄仁勇、姚大宁等5位武状元，其中朱可贞是顺德人，姚大宁是南海人。

（一）明代武状元朱可贞

朱可贞（生卒年不详），籍贯顺德龙江，臂力过人，能挽强弓，百发百中，又善使大刀，出神入化。

明天启四年（1624）进京会试成武进士，殿试第一甲第一名武状元及第，授锦衣副千户，历升中都副留守、封昭将军。做事直道而行，曾调任广东负责清剿海盗。

（二）清代武状元姚大宁

姚大宁（1772—1807），南海和顺镇文教乡人。

清嘉庆四年（1799）应举，考中第一名成武状元，获赐头等侍卫服和黄金甲铠等，衣锦还乡。

姚大宁穿过的官服（照片源自佛山市博物馆）
Official robe worn by Yao Daning (photo from Foshan Museum)

（三）地方文献对佛山历代武科名人的记载

清康熙《南海县志》载明代武举人李世勋等25人；清代武进士关麟、李圣龙2人，武举人邝廷宾等54人。

清道光《南海县志》载武举人张曰瑚等36人。

清宣统《南海县志》载武进士程以俊等4人、武举人陈龙韬等27人。

清嘉庆二十四年（1819）《三水县志》载武进士林盛1人、武举人吴日成等32人。

民国《佛山忠义乡志》载佛山历代武进士李圣龙等3人、武举人冼中振等42人。

民国时期，佛山考入武备学堂等的有陈天璜等123人。

从上可见佛山尚武之风的繁盛面貌。

period (1799) of the Qing Dynasty and came first in the examination, and was thus conferred the title of Martial Champion. He was awarded a first-class bodyguard uniform and a gold armor, winning high honors and social recognition for his hometown.

III. Foshan celebrities in imperial martial examinations in local records

According to *Nanhai County Chronicle* of the Kangxi period of the Qing Dynasty, there were 25 provincial graduates in imperial martial examinations including Li Shixun in the Ming Dynasty; and there were 2 metropolitan graduates, Guan Lin and Li Shenglong, and 54 provincial graduates including Kuang Tingbin in the Qing Dynasty.

According to *Nanhai County Chronicle* of the Daoguang period of the Qing Dynasty, there were 36 provincial graduates, including Zhang Yuehu.

According to *Nanhai County Chronicle* of the Xuantong period of the Qing Dynasty, there were 4 metropolitan graduates including Cheng Yijun and 27 provincial graduates including Chen Longtao.

According to *Sanshui County Chronicle* of the 24th year of the Jiaqing period (1819) of the Qing Dynasty, there was one metropolitan graduate called Lin Sheng, and 32 provincial graduates including Wu Richeng.

According to *Chronicle of Foshan, the Town of Loyalty and Righteousness* published in the Republic of China, there were 3 metropolitan graduates including Li Shenglong, and 42 provincial graduates including Xian Zhongzhen.

In the period of the Republic of China, Chen Tianhuang and another 122 people in Foshan were admitted to the military academy.

It can be seen from the above that martial spirit has been popular in Foshan.

1.6 Heaven and Earth Society and Development of Foshan Martial Arts

In the late Ming and early Qing dynasties, the Heaven and Earth Society (Hongmen) was active in China. It originated from the "Han Liu"[1] movement, launched by Yin Hungsing, a patriot rebelling against the Qing Dynasty. After Yin's death in an anti-Qing movement, his son turned to Zheng Chenggong for help. The thoughts of "Han Liu" spread to Zheng and his followers. Developed by Chen Jinnan, an official of Dongning Zongzhi, a government post in the late Ming Dynasty, the movement was later transformed into Hongmen, aimed at resisting the persecution of the Qing Dynasty and preserving the Han culture, which had become the keynote of this organization. Therefore, the later generations regarded Chen Jinnan as the founding father of Hongmen.

The special economic and military position of Foshan and the folk martial spirit attracted anti-Qing patriots, who thronged there to develop anti-Qing underground organizations, making Foshan one of the most important bases of the Heaven and Earth Society in the Qing Dynasty.

During the Yongzheng period (1722-1735) of the Qing Dynasty, Zhang Wu, a famous Peking Opera artist, came to Foshan and taught martial arts in theatrical troupes in order to spread the thought of opposing the Qing and restoring the Ming.

In the fourth year of the Xianfeng period (1854) of the Qing Dynasty, instigated by the Heaven and Earth Society, a peasant uprising led by Chen Kai and Li

1 "Han Liu" meaning retaining the Han nationality, rule or culture.

第六节　天地会与佛山武术发展

明末清初，天地会（洪门）组织在全国各地十分活跃。洪门起源于“汉留”[1]。“汉留”由抗清义士殷洪盛发起，殷洪盛抗清牺牲后，其子投奔郑成功，“汉留”构想传至郑成功所部。“汉留”经由南明东宁总制使陈近南发展，转化为洪门，旨在反抗清廷迫害及统治，留存汉族文化，故后人尊陈近南为洪门始祖。

佛山独特的经济和军事地位及民间尚武的风气引起各地反清志士的重视，于是纷纷潜入佛山发展反清秘密组织。佛山为天地会的重要根据地之一。

雍正年间，京剧名伶张五（摊手五）来到佛山，在戏班中教授武功，宣传反清复明思想。

清咸丰四年（1854），在天地会策动下，陈开、李文茂领导的农民起义爆发，“据说参加起义的以佛山、石湾四万多手工业工人和四乡农民，佛山琼花会馆戏行的数千粤剧艺人和九十多条船的船民，以及水上运输工人为基本队伍。……佛山成了广东起义军坚固的根据地，顺德、新会、清远、花县、龙门等地农民纷纷响应，附

1　“汉留”意为汉家保护或保护汉家天下或文化。

仗者数十万人”[1]。相传，清咸丰元年（1851）在佛山设立鸿胜馆的蔡李佛拳师张炎也投身运动之中。

天地会在广东的发展以及反清志士的南下，对广东武术的发展起到巨大的促进作用。

清代中后期至民国初期，多个拳种和武术组织在佛山发展壮大，名家辈出，民间习武热情空前高涨，佛山成为中国南派武术的中心。外来拳种结合佛山当地地理、气候条件和居民性格、体质，经过多年演变，形成了我们今天所看到的多种不同风格的拳械套路。

1 刘双慈：《粤剧与红领巾起义》，载佛山市政协文史资料委员会、佛山市文化局合编《佛山文史资料（第八辑）》，南海系列印刷公司1988年版。

Wenmao broke out. "It is said that the rebels mainly included more than 40,000 craftsmen and peasants in Foshan and Shiwan, thousands of Cantonese Opera artists of Qionghua Guild in Foshan, and boatmen and porters in over 90 boats....Foshan became the solid base of the Guangdong rebel army. Peasants in Shunde, Xinhui, Qingyuan, Huaxian (now Huadu District in Guangzhou), Longmen and other places answered the call one after another, and finally, there were hundreds of thousands of followers." [1] Legend has it that Zhang Yan, a master of Cai Li Fo Quan (Literally meaning "fist") who set up Hungsing Hall in the first year of the Xianfeng Period (1851) of the Qing Dynasty, also devoted himself to the movement.

The development of the Heaven and Earth Society in Guangdong and the southward movement of anti-Qing patriots have greatly promoted the advancement of martial arts in Guangdong.

From the mid and late Qing Dynasty to the early Republic of China, the development of various martial arts styles and organizations in Foshan produced numerous masters and resulted in ever higher enthusiasm for martial arts among the people, turning Foshan into the center of Southern martial arts in China. The exotic martial arts styles, combined with local geographical and climatic conditions, and residents' personalities and physique, have formed their own styles over the years.

1 Liu Shuangci, "Cantonese Opera and the Red Scart Rebellion" Artist Li Wenmao, in *Foshan Cultural and Historical Accounts (Volume 8)*, eds. Foshan CPPCC Cultural and Historical Date Committee. Foshan Cultural Bureau, Nanhai Xilie Printing Co., 1988.

FOSHAN, CHINA

第二章

清代传入佛山的拳种及其发展

Chapter 2

Martial Arts Types Introduced into Foshan in the Qing Dynasty and their Development

民间武术在佛山发展迅猛，清代广东南拳五大名拳（洪拳、刘家拳、蔡家拳、李家拳、莫家拳）中以洪拳名声最盛，名家辈出。蔡李佛拳从广东新会传入，在多次社会变革中发挥了重要作用。咏春拳与粤剧有着紧密联系，是当今佛山流派分支繁盛、拳馆建立众多的拳种。清末民初出现的南家拳、周家拳，如今仍在传播发展。

Folk martial arts have developed rapidly in Foshan. Among the five famous Southern martial arts types introduced into Foshan in the Qing Dynasty, (namely, Hong Quan, Liu jia Quan, Cai jia Quan, Li jia Quan, and Mo jiaquan), Hong Quan enjoys the greatest reputation and numerous masters. Cai Li Fo Quan, introduced from Xinhui, Guangdong has played an important role in various social transformations. Yongchun Quan, which is closely related to the Cantonese Opera, has large numbers of branches and martial arts halls in Foshan. Nan Jia Quan and Zhou Jia Quan which emerged at the end of the Qing Dynasty and the early Republic of China are still developing in the city.

2.1 Hong Quan

I. Origin of Hong Quan

Hong Quan, a kind of traditional Southern martial arts in China, was created by combining the movements and characteristics of dragons, snakes, tigers, leopards, cranes, lions, elephants, horses, monkeys and Asiatic golden cats with martial arts techniques. It features rich hand movements, few leg movements, earnest steps, hard bridge-shaped hand movements and horse stances, strength and vigor, and the use of *qi* (literally meaning "air" or "breath") and sound.
The Southern martial arts are extensively believed to have originated from the Southern Shaolin Temple in Fujian. The Southern martial arts in Fujian, Guangdong and Hubei, including Hong Quan, Liu Jia Quan, Cai Jia Quan, Li Jia Quan and Mo Jia Quan were all imparted by the five monks of the Southern Shaolin Temple, who were revered as the "Five Ancestors of the Southern Martial Arts". The Southern martial arts are also believed to have originated from the Heaven and Earth Society.

II. Famous masters of Hong Quan in Foshan in the Qing Dynasty

Representatives of Hong Quan in Foshan included Tie Qiao San, Lin Fucheng, Lu Yacai, Wang Yinlin, and Huang Qiying in the mid to late Qing Dynasty, and Huang Feihong and Lin Shirong in the late Qing Dynasty and the early Republic of China. There are other Hong Quan organizations in the different districts of Foshan.

第一节　洪拳

（一）洪拳起源

洪拳为中国传统拳术中的南拳之一，由龙、蛇、虎、豹、鹤、狮、象、马、猴、彪的象形与特性结合武术技法创编而成。风格特点：手法丰富，腿法较少，步趋热烈，硬桥硬马，刚劲有力，以气催力，以声助威。

关于南拳的起源，流传最广泛的说法是来自福建南少林寺。福建、广东、湖北一带的南拳，包括洪拳、刘家拳、蔡家拳、李家拳、莫家拳，都由南少林寺5位僧人传出，这5位僧人被世人尊为“南拳五祖”。民间也有南拳来自天地会的说法。

（二）清代佛山洪拳主要名家

洪拳代表人物铁桥三、林福成、陆亚采、王隐林、黄麒英等活跃于清代中晚期，黄飞鸿、林世荣等活跃于清末民初。目前，在佛山各区仍有其他脉络的洪拳组织。

洪拳
Hong Quan

Tie Qiao San (1813-1886), originally named Liang Kun, was a native of Nanhai County, Guangdong Province. Keen on martial arts, he started learning from masters since young. At Nengren Temple in the Baiyun Mountain in Guangzhou, he met Monk Jueyin from the Shaolin Temple in Putian, Fujian, learned from him for seven years and mastered all the skills. Tie Qiao San was the first representative of Hong Quan after its introduction into Guangdong and the top of the "Ten Tigers" in the late Qing Dynasty. He had amazing arm strength and was renowned for his steady bridge hands and horse stances, outstanding skills and righteousness. Among his numerous students, Lin Fucheng was the most outstanding.

Lin Fucheng (years of birth and death unknown), was a native of Foshan. He taught Huang Feihong Iron Wire Fist and Flying Stone Stunt.

III. Huang Feihong, a great master of Hong Quan

Huang Feihong, a great master of Hong Quan was a typical representative of the spirit and image of Southern martial arts. Huang is a household name with far-reaching influences.

Huang's life story was first made known by *A Supplementary Biography of Huang Feihong* compiled in 1933 by Zhu Yuzhai, a student of Lin Shirong's. Since then, different versions of novels have been carried in newspapers in instalments. Since the 1950s and 1960s, more than 100 cultural products on Huang Feihong in the form of broadcasts, TV serials and films have been produced.

Huang Feihong (1856-1925) was from Luzhou Village, Xiqiao, Nanhai. When he was six, he started learning martial arts from his father and learned Tiger and Crane Double Pattern Set, I-shaped Tiger Subduing Fist, Five-Element Fist, and Eight-Diagram Pole Fighting. Huang earned a living in Guangzhou and Foshan by performing martial arts and selling medicine. Later, he learned Iron Wire Fist and Flying Stone Stunt from Lin Fucheng, a distinguished student of Tie Qiao San's. He also learned Eight-point Arrow Fist from Ye Dacheng and Shadowless Kicks from Song Huitang. He formed his own unique style by integrating what he had learned from different martial arts masters.

铁桥三（1813—1886），原名梁坤，广东南海县人。年幼时就爱好武术，到处寻访名师。在广州白云山能仁寺，遇见来自福建莆田少林寺的觉因和尚，在其门下带发修行7年，尽得真传。铁桥三为洪拳传入广东后第一位代表人物，晚清广东“十虎”之首。他臂力惊人，以桥马沉雄著称，马步四平八稳，武艺超群。他行侠仗义，徒弟甚多，林福成是其中的佼佼者。

林福成（生卒年不详），佛山人，以铁线拳法和飞砣绝技授黄飞鸿。

（三）洪拳一代宗师黄飞鸿

黄飞鸿像（照片来自佛山市博物馆）
Photo of Huang Feihong (provided by Foshan Museum)

黄飞鸿是洪拳一代宗师，是南派武术精神形象的典型代表，家喻户晓，影响深远。

其生平事迹传播，最早见于1933年林世荣徒弟朱愚斋编撰的《黄飞鸿别传》，之后，出现多种版本的小说，通过报刊连载展示。二十世纪五六十年代以来，香港电台广播、电视连续剧、电影等以黄飞鸿为题材的文化产品有100多部。

黄飞鸿（1856—1925），祖籍南海西樵禄舟村。6岁开始随父亲黄麒英习武，学得洪拳之虎鹤双形拳、工字伏虎拳、五形拳、五郎八卦棍等。常在佛山、广州等地行走江湖，以演艺卖药为生。后在佛山拜铁桥三的

In 1873, the 17-year-old Huang started teaching students at Qifu Shuijiao, Guangzhou, who were mainly workers of the copper or iron industry. He also taught martial arts at Three Stalls Market (stalls of fruits, vegetables and fish).

Since 1878, he ran an orthopedic clinic near the Huilan Brige, Xiguan, Guangzhou and served as an armed escort at the Cricket Ground run by Lu Jiushu at the Pingzheng Bridge, Foshan.

In 1886, Huang Feihong's father Huang Qiying passed away. Huang Feihong set up Baozhilin Pharmacy on Ren'an Street, Guangzhou. Because of his superb medical skills to treat fractures and bruises, he was considered a wonder at that time. He also taught Hong Quan and served as the head coach of fighting in the armies of Wu Quanmei and Liu Yongfu. He also went with Liu Yongfu to Taiwan to fight against the Japanese agression.

In the late Qing Dynasty and the early Republic of China, Huang Feihong was already a famous Hong Quan master and was often invited to demonstrate martial arts at temple fairs or celebration activities. In 1894, he performed together with Lin Shirong, Cheng Hua, Huang Manrong, Zhang Ju, Baitoubao and Liang Xisu in Xiguan, Guangzhou and demonstrated Iron Wire Fist. During his lifetime, he taught numerous students, among whom were Liang Kuan and Lin Shirong.

In August 1924, the Canton Merchant Volunteers Corps Uprising took place and Ren'an Street was on fire. His painstakingly-run Baozhilin was destroyed. He was deeply depressed and fell ill.

In 1925, Huang Feihong passed away at Fangbian (Convenience) Hospital in Guangzhou at the age of 69.

Huang Feihong had four marriages. Among his four sons, Hanshen who had learned his skills best was killed. Feihong regretted that and never taught his other three sons martial arts, so they all became businessmen instead. In his family, it was Mo Guilan, his fourth wife, who mastered most of his skills.

Mo Guilan was a native of Gaozhou, Guangdong Province. She started practicing martial arts from a young age and mastered Mo Jia Quan well, so she was a heroine. She was married to Huang Feihong because of martial arts.

After Huang Feihong's death, Mo Guilan taught at the Women's Section of

高徒林福成为师，学得铁线拳法、飞砣绝技。又师从叶大成学习八分箭拳，从宋辉镗学得无影脚。他将所学技艺融会贯通，形成独特风格。

1873年，17岁的黄飞鸿在广州第七甫水脚设馆授徒，从学者多为铜、铁行工人，又在三栏行（三栏指果栏、菜栏、鱼栏）传授武术。

1878年起在广州西关回澜桥附近设跌打医馆，同时在佛山平政桥卢九叔开设的蟀场担任保镖。

1886年，黄飞鸿之父黄麒英去世。黄飞鸿在广州豆栏仁安街开设“宝芝林”药局，悬壶济世。他医术精湛，驳骨疗伤之技时称一绝。他兼教洪拳，先后任吴全美部、刘永福部军中技击总教练，随刘永福赴台湾抗击日本侵略者。

黄飞鸿在清末民初时期为广东洪拳名家，常应邀为庙会贺诞或庆典活动做武术演示，1894年曾与林世荣、程华、黄满荣、张居、白头保、梁细苏等在广州西关同台献技，展示铁线拳。一生授徒无数，嫡传弟子有梁宽、林世荣等。

1924年8月，广州商团暴动，仁安街遭大火，黄飞鸿苦心经营的“宝芝林”毁于一旦。他深受打击，郁闷成疾。

1925年，黄飞鸿在广州方便医院去世，享年69岁。

黄飞鸿结过4次婚。四子中，以汉深最得其技艺真传，惜被害身亡，飞鸿悔恨之，从此不再传其他儿子武功。余三子，皆以营商为业。家中终得其真传者，为四夫人莫桂兰。

莫桂兰，高州人。自小喜爱习武，早年学习莫家拳，根基扎实，为巾帼英雄。她与黄飞鸿也是因武结缘。

Yiyongtang Martial Arts Gymnasium.

In 1946, Mo Guilan moved to Hong Kong. She first made a living at Gloucester Road, putting up the signboard "Mo Guilan, wife of Huang Feihong, excelling in treating fractures and bruises". Later she set up Huang Feihong Martial Arts Society, and then Huang Feihong Fitness College on Lockhat Road which was later moved to Causeway Bay.

黃飛鴻師傅傳

黃漢熙

鴻師傅傳

1957年《香港商报》所载的《黄飞鸿师傅传》（照片源自佛山市博物馆）

"A Biography of Huang Feihong" carried in *Hong Kong Commercial Daily* in 1957 (photo provided by Foshan Museum)

On November 3rd, 1982, Mo Guilan passed away in Hong Kong.

Of Hong Quan passed down from Huang Feihong, the main freehand fighting routines include I-shaped Tiger Subduing Fist, Tiger and Crane Double Pattern Set, Five-Element Fist, and Iron Wire Fist; while main weapon routines include Spring and Autumn Broadswords, Double Flying Stones, Mother-and-Son Twin Swords, Eight-Diagram Pole Fighting, Swords Stained with Plum Blossoms, Walker Sticks and Shadowless Kicks.

IV. Lin Shirong, an important disseminator of Hong Quan

Lin Shirong (1861-1943) was a native of Xihe Village, Pingzhou, Nanhai, Guangdong.

Since his early childhood, Lin learned his family martial arts techniques including Moon Swords, Gilt Griddles and Butterfly Palms from his uncle Lin Boshan. Later he learned Six-Point-Five Club and Arrow-Palm Abacus Fist from Hu Jinxing and Zhong Hongshan, two great Hong Quan masters.

In 1883, the 23-year-old Lin Shirong became a student of Huang Feihong's and

林世荣演示洪拳（孔祥辉供图）

Lin Shirong demonstrating Hong Quan (photo provided by Kong Xianghui)

followed Huang for over 20 years, thus becoming the inheritor of the Huang Feihong Style Hong Quan.

In 1905 when he was 45 years old, Lin set up martial arts gymnasiums at the Huilan Bridge, Chentang, Baohuafang, Xinqiaoshi, the Kong Clan Academy, Maima Street and Guangya Hall of Guangzhou [1]. Being frank, warm-hearted and righteous, he often fought against the bandits.

In the early Republic of China, he was employed by Li Fulin, commander of the "Fu (fortune) Army" as a martial arts coach.

In 1921, he performed martial arts for charity fundraising for an orphanage in Guangzhou and was awarded a Silver Medal by Dr. Sun Yat-sen.

Later Lin made his living in Hong Kong. Apart from teaching Hong Quan at Wan Chai and Central, he also taught at meat shops and Chen Zibao School.

In the early 1930s, Lin established the Nanwu Athletic Federation and served as the head coach of Martial Arts. There were over 10,000 students. When Hong Kong was occupied by Japan during the War of Resistance against Japanese Aggression, Lin went back to live in seclusion in his hometown Pingzhou, Nanhai.

Since 1930, in order to promote martial arts, apart from teaching, Lin Shirong also compiled a number of martial arts manuals including *I-shaped Tiger Subduing Fist*, *Iron Wire Fist and Tiger* and *Crane Double Pattern Set*, which have had far-reaching influences at home and abroad.

In 1943, he passed away at the age of 83.

1 Wei Shaobo. "A Brief Account of Mr. Lin Shirong", in *Illustrations of I-shaped Tiger Subduing Fist of Lin Shirong*, 1936.

黄飞鸿去世后，莫桂兰在义勇堂武馆女子部任教。

1946年，莫桂兰移居香港，先在告士打道挂出“黄飞鸿授妻莫桂兰精医跌打”招牌谋生，继后开设“黄飞鸿国术社”，又在骆克道开设“黄飞鸿健身学院”，后迁往铜锣湾。

1982年11月3日，莫桂兰于香港逝世。

黄飞鸿所传洪拳中，主要徒手拳术有工字伏虎拳、虎鹤双形拳、五形拳、铁线拳、无影脚等，主要器械套路有春秋大刀、双飞砣、子母双刀、五郎八卦棍、十字梅花剑、行者棒等。

（四）洪拳重要传播者林世荣

林世荣（1861—1943），广东南海平洲西河村人。自幼随伯父林伯善学习家传武术行月刀、流金铛和蝴蝶掌，又先后师从胡金星、钟洪山两位洪拳名师，学得六点半棍和箭掌算盘拳等。

1883年，23岁的林世荣带艺入门，拜黄飞鸿为师，师从黄飞鸿20多年，成为黄飞鸿洪拳法的衣钵传人。

1905年，45岁的林世荣在广州回澜桥、陈塘、宝华坊、新桥市、孔家祠、卖麻街、光雅堂等地设立武馆[1]。他性格爽直，行侠仗义，常为民出头惩治奸恶。

民国初年，受“福军”军长李福林所聘，担任国术教官。

1 韦少伯：《林世荣先生略历》，载《林世荣工字伏虎拳图说》，1936年版。

1921年，在广州为孤儿院慈善筹款进行武术表演，获孙中山颁发银质奖章。

后到香港谋生，除在湾仔、中环等地教授洪拳外，先后在香港肉行、陈子褒学校等处任教。

20世纪30年代初，创设南武体育会，担任国术总教练，门下弟子万余人。抗日战争时期，香港沦陷，回家乡南海平洲隐居。

1934年香港林世荣国术团全体同人拍照纪念（林镇成供图）

Lin Shirong Martial Arts Society in Hong Kong in 1934 (photo provided by Lam Chun Sing)

1930年后，为弘扬国术，授徒之余整理出《工字伏虎拳》《铁线拳》《虎鹤双形拳》等拳谱，在海内外影响巨大。

1943年去世，时年83岁。

（五）洪拳代表性套路

1. 虎鹤双形拳

虎鹤双形拳由黄飞鸿传林世荣。虎形练气与力，动作沉雄，声威叱咤，有龙腾虎跃之势；鹤形练精与神，身手灵捷、动作

洪拳
Hong Quan

V. Representative routines of Hong Quan

1. Tiger and Crane Double Pattern Set

Tiger and Crane Double Pattern Set was passed from Huang Feihong to Lin Shirong. The tiger patterns train energy and strength. The movements are steady and strong, accompanied by powerful shouts, just like flying dragons and leaping tigers. The crane patterns train essence and spirit. The movements are agile, fast, calm and restful. The Tiger and Crane Double Pattern Set is the representative of the Huang Feihong Style Martial Arts.

2. I-shaped Tiger Subduing Fist

I-shaped Tiger Subduing Fist is a basic skill of Hong Quan. It got its name because the forward and backward movements form the letter "I". It features steady stances, powerful hand movements, close fist approaches, and well-regulated forward and backward movements. It is the basis for learning other martial arts types and weapons. Everyone who wanted to become a student of Huang Feihong's must learn this to steady their stances, consolidate their hand movements and correct their steps.

VI. Technical styles of Hong Quan

Hong Quan requires straightened upper parts, steady steps and sturdy lower parts.

The hand patterns include fists, palms, fingers, claws, hooks and crane-top hands. The hand movements include the sinking bridge, circling bridge, sealing bridge, punching fists and thrusting palms.

The step patterns are mainly four level horses, supplemented by triangular horses, centerline horses, hanging horses and Xicheng steps.

The body patterns require a slightly drawn-in chest, a straightened waist, a drawn-in abdomen, contracted hips, sunken shoulders, drooping elbows, sinking bridges and sitting stances.

When striking, one is required to kick the legs, buckle the knees, close the hips, and turn the waist. Energy accumulation comes before striking. Sometimes actions are accompanied by shouts to enhance the effect.

The different schools of Hong Quan are consistent in the overall style though they may have different characteristics in the dissemination process.

VII. The status quo of Hong Quan

There was a proverb that "where there are ancestral halls, there are lion dancing and Hong Quan". Though Hong Quan is still inherited in the different districts of Foshan, it seems to lack vitality and integrated power, so there is still a long way to go for its inheritance.

1. Huang Feihong and Lin Shirong's Sect

(1) Lam Chun Sing Martial Arts and Dragon Lion Training Base of Hong Kong (China) International Hong Quan Headquarter

The founder of Hong Kong (China) International Hong Quan Headquarter was Lam Chun Sing.

Lam Chun Sing was born in Hong Kong in 1952 and lived in Wan Chai. At the age of six, he started learning Hong Quan from his father and was skilled at using swords, spears, sabers and halberds.

迅速，有气定神闲之妙，故称虎鹤双形拳，为黄飞鸿一门之代表拳法。

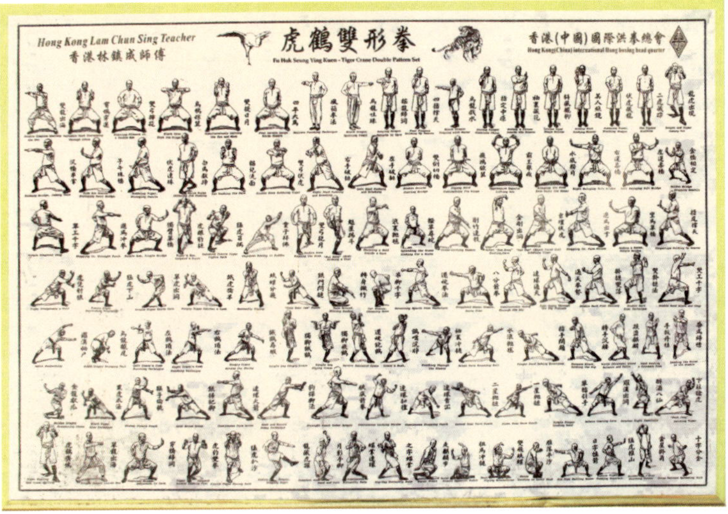

林世荣的“虎鹤双形拳”演示图（林镇成供图）
The illustration of Tiger and Crane Double Pattern Set of Lin Shirong (photo provided by Lam Chun Sing)

2. 工字伏虎拳

工字伏虎拳，为洪拳的基本拳法，以步进退成“工”字形，故得名。工字伏虎拳腰马稳健，桥手刚劲，法门紧密，进退有规，是学习其他拳术、器械的基础。凡入黄飞鸿门下者，必先习此拳以稳健腰马，坚实桥手，正步法。

（六）洪拳技术风格

洪拳要求身正步稳，下盘沉实。

手形有拳、掌、指、爪、勾、鹤顶手等。手法有沉桥、圈桥、封桥、冲拳、插掌等。

步形以四平马为主，还有三角马、子午马、吊马和熙城步等。

身形要求含胸、立腰、收腹、敛臀、沉肩、垂肘、沉桥坐步。

发力时要求蹬腿、扣膝、合胯、转腰，先蓄后发，猛力出击。有时还因势发声，以声助威。

洪拳各家总体风格一致，传承过程中或各有特色。

（七）洪拳传承现状

昔日民谚谓“只要有祠堂，就会有狮子和洪拳”，而目前洪拳在佛山各个区域虽有传承，但面临青黄不接之境况，没有形成较好的整合力量，要弘扬发展，任重而道远。

1. 黄飞鸿、林世荣一脉

（1）香港（中国）国际洪拳总会林镇成武术龙狮训练基地

香港（中国）国际洪拳总会创办人是林镇成。

林镇成1952年出生于香港，家住湾仔。6岁随父学习洪拳，刀、枪、剑、戟无所不能。

2011年，林镇成返回家乡南海，创办“林世荣、林祖、林镇成武术龙狮训练基地”，这是香港（中国）国际洪拳总会现时在国内唯一

林镇成在海外传播洪拳（林镇成供图）
Lam Chun Sing spreading Hong Quan abroad (photo provided by Lam Chun Sing)

In 2011, Lam Chun Sing returned to his hometown Nanhai and established "Lin Shirong, Lin Zu and Lam Chun Sing Dragon Lion Training Base", the only training base of Hong Kong (China) International Hong Quan Headquarter in Chinese mainland. It's currently located at Mai Qiufang Memorial Hall in the Mai Ancestral Hall in Diejiao, Nanhai.

Lam Chun Sing is now the head of Hong Kong (China) International Hong Quan Headquarter. He has been teaching martial arts for over 40 years, with numerous students around the world.

Hong Quan taught by Lam Chun Sing includes over 40 freehand fighting and weapon routines and Southern lion dancing skills, such as the Three Treasures of Hong Quan (I-shaped Tiger Subduing Fist, Tiger and Crane Double Pattern Set and Iron Wire Fist), Five-Element Fist, Ten-Element Fist, Fighting Palms (also called "Arrow Palms"), Liu Jia Quan, Mantis Fist, sparring of Tiger and Crane Double Pattern Set, sparring of I-shaped Tiger Subduing Fist; Eight-Diagram Pole Fighting, Butterfly Double Swords, Double-Blade Swords, Long Benches, Walker Sticks, the Yao Rakes, Plum Blossom Spears, Kunlun Sabers, Double Swords versus Spears, Double Whips, and Single Whips.

(2) Kong Xianghui Martial Arts Sport Association

Kong Xianghui Martial Arts Sport Association was established in 2012 by Kong Xianghui, an extended student of Huang Feihong and Lin Shirong's School of

Hong Quan.

Kong Xianghui, born in 1948, is from Diejiao, Guicheng, Nanhai, Foshan. He started practicing martial arts since young.

When he was five, he started to learn Southern School Hong Quan from his uncle Kong Qi, a Hong Quan master at Bilin Hall.

In 1979, he moved to Hong Kong. In 1982, he began to follow Lin Zu, a son of Lin Shirong's to further improve his Hong Quan skills. He practiced there for 30 years.

In 2012, Kong, after retirement, returned to live in his hometown Nanhai where he self-financed the Kong Xianghui Martial Arts Sport Association and taught children and young people there the skills of Hong Quan and lion dancing for free.

2. Tan Min's Sect

(1) Nanhai Beisha Martial Arts Gymnasium

The most outstanding characteristic of this gymnasium is the White Eyebrow Fist. It also has a solid foundation of Hong Quan. Founded by Tan Min and Hu Zhongxian, the gymnasium has branches and well over 3,000 students at its prime time.

It is said that Zen Master Zhishan of Fujian Shaolin Temple passed his skills to Lu Yacai, who had two famous students in Guangdong. One was Liang Kun, and the other was Huang Tai. Tie Qiao San passed his skills to Tan Min, who taught He An, Hu Zhongxian and Lin Fucheng.

Both Tan Min and Hu Zhongxian were from Shilong, Shenshan, Huaxian, Guangdong.

Tan Min's father was rich and often donated money to Heshun Jinshan Temple and had the chance to know Tie Qiao San, who was active in Sanshui. So Tan Min became Tie Qiao San's student and mastered magical skills such as Iron Bridge and Horse Falling to Take Root.

Hu Zhongxian was also a mighty figure in Huaxian. He used to be the captain of the Broadsword Team, which safeguarded the security of Guangzhou-Huangxian Railway.

Hu Zhongxian and He An learned Iron Wire Fist and Three-Wire Fist from Tan

的武术龙狮训练基地，现址在南海叠滘麦氏宗祠的麦秋芳纪念堂。

林镇成现任香港（中国）国际洪拳总会会长，授徒40余年，门下弟子遍布世界各地，桃李盈门。

林镇成所教授的洪拳包括洪拳三宝（工字伏虎拳、虎鹤双形拳、铁线拳）、五行拳、十形拳、战掌（又称“箭掌”）、刘家拳、崩步、虎鹤双形拳对练、工字伏虎拳对练，以及五郎八卦棍、蝴蝶双刀、大行双叶刀、横头凳、行者棒、瑶家大耙、梅花缨枪、昆仑剑、双刀对缨枪、双鞭、单鞭等40多套拳械套路和南派醒狮技艺。

（2）孔祥辉国术体育会

孔祥辉国术体育会由黄飞鸿、林世荣系洪拳再传弟子孔祥辉于2012年创办。

孔祥辉，1948年出生，为佛山南海桂城叠滘人，自幼习武。

5岁开始跟随伯父、比麟堂洪拳师傅孔其先生习练南派洪拳。

1979年移居香港，1982年拜师林世荣嗣子林祖门下，进一步深造洪拳技法30年。

2012年，孔师傅退休后返回南海桂城叠滘居住，自筹资金开办孔祥辉国术体育会，义务教授乡中青少年洪拳及醒狮等技法。

2. 谭敏一脉

（1）南海北沙武术馆

该馆当今最具特色的是白眉拳教习，而洪拳更是根基深厚。创始人为谭敏、胡忠贤。弟子众多，下设分馆，鼎盛时弟子有3000多人。

据传，福建少林至善禅师传艺给陆亚采，陆亚采在广东有两位比较出名的徒弟，一位是梁坤，另一位是黄泰。铁桥三传艺给谭敏，谭敏传徒何安、胡忠贤和林福成。

谭敏和胡忠贤都是广东花县神山石龙人。

谭敏的父亲家境优渥，经常捐资给和顺金山寺，故有机缘认识铁桥三。铁桥三在三水一带活动，谭敏拜铁桥三为师，得其衣钵，练出“铁桥”“马落生根”等功夫。

胡忠贤在花县也是个威猛人物，曾任大刀队队长，负责带领队员保卫广花铁路安全。

胡忠贤和何安拜谭敏为师，学习谭家铁线拳、三线拳。由于胡忠贤之妻是谭敏的侄女，因而胡忠贤与谭敏关系很密切。胡忠贤学艺很精，创立了胡家铁线拳和具有个人风格的三线拳。当时社会上流行谭家和胡家铁线、三线（展）两种套路，据闻两种套路其实手法一致，只是步法各异。

民国时期，在谭敏的指导下，胡忠贤在广州西关文昌路文昌街设立“胡忠贤武馆”（民间称“胡馆”）。胡忠贤任馆长，何安为助教。胡馆当时聘请了许多名师，洪拳、蔡李佛拳、白眉拳、龙形拳等均有专人传授。

南海一带的武术教头，大多是胡馆门下弟子，北沙有黄卓、谭胡等，广州有何少祺等，传播范围广，有一定名气。

（2）梁氏洪拳国术馆

该馆位于南海平洲玉器街商铺二楼文化中心，由梁荫邦于2007年11月19日创办。

Min. As Hu's wife was Tan's niece, Hu and Tan maintained close contacts. Hu learned well and established the Hu Iron Wire Fist and Three-Wire Fist with a personal style. At that time, both Tan's and Hu's routines of Iron Wire Fist and Three-Wire Fist were popular in society. It is said that the two had the same hand movements but different movements of the feet.

During the Republic of China, under the guidance of Tan Min, Hu Zhongxian established the "Hu Zhongxian Martial Arts Gymnasium" (popularly called "the Hu Gymnasium") on Wenchang Street, Xiguan, Guangzhou. Hu Zhongxian was the head while He An was a teaching assistant. The gymnasium employed a lot of great martial artists to teach Hong Quan, Cai Li Fo Quan, White Eyebrow Fist, and Dragon Style Fist.

Most martial arts coaches in Nanhai have been students of the Hu Gymnasium, such as Huang Zhuo and Tan Hu in Beisha; and He Shaoqi in Guangzhou. The Hu Gymnasium has spread widely and enjoyed certain fame.

(2) The Liang's Hong Quan Martial Arts Gymnasium

Located in the Cultural Center on the 2nd floor of Yuqi Street Shopping Mall, Pingzhou, Nanhai, the gymnasium was established by Liang Yinbang on November 19th, 2007.

Liang Yinbang was born in 1946. His father Liang Xin (1913-1983) was a student of Lyu Jian's, who was an inheritor of Hu Zhongxian Martial Arts Gymnasium of Tan Min's Sect of Hong Quan.

Liang Xin was originally from Dachong, Lishui, Nanhai and was nicknamed "Dwarf Xin". In Guangzhou he was acquainted with Lyu Jian and learned Hong Quan from him. Because of his diligence, Liang Xin learned all the skills and became Lyu's teaching assistant. "Dwarf Xin" of Hong Quan was quite famous in the local area.

In 1945, Liang Xin was invited to teach martial arts at Xiajiao Village, Pingzhou, Nanhai.

Liang Yinbang has inherited his father Liang Xin's skills, including martial arts, lion dancing and orthopedic medicine.

At the age of eight, Liang Yinbang started to learn Hong Quan from his father. When he was a student at Nanhai No.1 Middle School, he was already a great performer of martial arts. His martial arts skills include Little Yanqing Fist, Little Cross Fist, Single Bow Tiger Subduing Fist, Forest-Crossing Swallow, Big-Step Plum Blossoms, Iron Bow Three Rollers, and Iron Rollers. Weapon routines include Walker Sticks (Double-Head Sticks), broadswords, Dragon Sabers, Long Benches, Tasseled Spears, and sparring. Auxiliary apparatuses of Hong Quan include iron rings and iron rods, which are quite different from others.

Liang Xin's students include Liang Yinbang, Liang Rongbang and others. Liang Yinbang's main students are Wu Ruquan and others.

3. Yan Zhenhua's Sect

In the past there were many gymnasiums of Yan Zhenhua's Sect of Hong Quan in Nanhai, including the headquarters and 34 branches.

Oral History of Xiqiao Martial Arts by Zhou Xiao records,

> Before the War of Resistance against Japanese Aggression, at the age of five or six, Yan Zhenhua went to Guangzhou with his father who was in the shoe business. He learned Hong Quan and lion dancing from Pan Di and Zhang Zhao.
>
> During the War, after fighting with the Japanese, he escaped from Guangzhou and first went to live in Xiaofengtian Village, Luocun, Nanhai. Later he went to teach martial arts at Xiqiao at the invitation of the villagers and became a resident there. So far this sect has a lot of branches.

4. Hong Quan Activity Center of Foshan Jingwu Sports Association

In the early days of its establishment, the Center mainly focused on spreading the Northern martial arts, supplemented with the Southern ones. It was after the resumption of the Association in 1986 that Hong Quan was taught. The first one to teach it within the organization was Peng Nan.

Peng Nan (1911-1995), was a native of Huaxian County, Guangdong Province, whose family lived in Foshan for generations. Because he had a large mole on his right face, he was called "Black Face Nan".

At the age of 13, he started learning martial arts from Gan Zhu, Pang Ling, Ma Fen, Wu Wenlong and Liang Xisu's student Chen Tian.

At the age of 36, after learning martial arts from Zhao Jiu, a great Yongchun master, he was enlightened by Li Yechi and mastered all the skills, which made

梁荫邦出生于1946年，其父梁新（1913—1983）师从吕坚，吕坚为洪拳谭敏一脉胡忠贤武馆传人。

梁新本为南海里水大涌人，人称“矮人新”。他在广州认识吕坚师傅，学得洪拳。由于梁新勤奋用功，尽得吕坚衣钵真传，并担任了他的助教。洪拳“矮人新”在当地颇有名气。

1945年，梁新受平洲夏滘村人邀请到当地教拳。

梁荫邦继承了父亲梁新的技艺，包括拳械、狮艺和跌打医术。

梁荫邦8岁开始随父亲学习洪拳，在南海一中读书时已是武术表演的能手。他所学拳术有小燕青拳、小十字拳、单弓伏虎拳、穿林燕、大步梅、铁弓三辗、铁辗；所学器械套路有行者棒（双头棍）、大刀、游龙剑、横头凳、缨枪，还有对练等；洪拳练功辅助器具有铁环、铁棍，与众不同。

梁新的徒弟除了梁荫邦，还有梁荣邦等。梁荫邦的主要徒弟有吴汝全等。

3. 颜振华一脉

颜振华一脉在南海设有多处洪拳武馆，过去曾包括1个总馆和34个分馆。

据周肖《西樵武林口述史》记录：

抗战前，颜振华五六岁时随父到广州经营鞋业。其间先后师从潘狄和张兆学习洪拳和狮艺。

抗战期间，与日本人交手后逃离广州。首先到南海罗村小丰田村居住，后受西樵村民之邀到当地传授武术，随之落籍西樵，传播至今，分支较多。

4. 佛山精武体育会洪拳活动中心

建立之初以传承北派武术为主，南拳辅之。明确有洪拳传播是在1986年复会之后，最早在会内传授洪拳的是彭南。

彭南（1911—1995），祖籍广东花县，世居佛山，因右脸有巴掌大的黑痣，人称“黑面南”。

13岁习武，先后师从甘珠、庞玲、马芬、伍文龙、梁细苏弟子陈添等。

36岁时随咏春名师招就习技后得黎叶篪指点，得其真传。其精湛的武艺在珠江三角洲一带享有盛誉。

晚年热心于佛山精武事业，积极参与对佛山武术的挖掘，开展传播活动，1994年荣获“广东武林百杰”称号。

彭南洪拳传统套路主要有铁环拳、铲马刀、蝴蝶双刀、双板斧、姚家大扒等。

2001年，彭南之子彭树藻、彭树松联同高建峰、廖智一、苏国明等在佛山精武体育会设立洪拳活动中心，广泛传播洪拳及南派传统狮艺。

5. 洪熙官一脉

2014年三水区非遗代表性项目“全胜堂”洪拳，以洪熙官一脉洪拳的传人为代表。

三水区洪拳代表性传承人洪永强介绍：清代乾隆年间，洪熙官在花县赤坭圩关帝庙传授洪拳，弟子有莲塘村骆日成、毕村毕海、朱村朱福、大华村关福、铁匠曾国礼等人。

其中，花县新民埠朱村的朱福（约1772—1852）是广东天地

him reputed in the Pearl River Delta.

In his twilight years, he actively participated in excavating and disseminating Foshan martial arts and was awarded as one of the "One Hundred Celebrities of Martial Arts in Guangdong".

The traditional routines of Peng Nan's Hong Quan mainly include Iron Ring Fists, Horse Shoveling Swords, Butterfly Double Swords, Double Axes, and the Yao Rakes.

In 2001, Peng Nan's sons Peng Shuzao and Peng Shusong, together with Gao Jianfeng, Liao Zhiyi and Su Guoming, jointly established Hong Quan Activity Center under Foshan Jingwu Sports Association to disseminate Hong Quan and traditional Southern lion dancing.

5. Hong Xiguan's Sect

"Quanshengtang" Hong Quan, an item in the List of Intangible Cultural Heritage of Sanshui District in 2014, is represented by Hong Xiguan's Sect.

According to Hong Yongqiang, a representative inheritor of Sanshui Hong Quan, during the Qianlong period of the Qing Dynasty, Hong Xiguan taught Hong Quan at Emperor Guan Temple in Chiniwei, Huaxian County. His students included Luo Richeng from Liantang Village, Bi Hai from Bicun Village, Zhu Fu from Zhucun Village, Guan Fu and blacksmith Zeng Guoli from Dahua Village.

Among them, Zhu Fu (c. 1772-1852), from Zhucun Village, Xinminbu, Huaxian County was one of the early core figures of Guangdong Heaven and Earth Society and took part in the revolt led by Chen Si (nicknamed "the Broken Shoe Four") of the Society's branch in Boluo, Huizhou in the seventh year of the Jiaqing period (1802) of the Qing Dynasty. After the failure of the revolt, he returned to Tanbu and Lixi of Huaxian County to teach Hong Quan.

Chen Jin'gang (1820-1865), originally named Chen Ze, was born in a poor family in Qinghu Village, Fanhu Town, Sanshui County. In his youth, he became a student in Quanshengtang Hong Quan Gymnasium established by Zhu Fu. Later the gymnasium was run by Zhu Fu's son Zhu Ziru. Disguised as a martial arts gymnasium, Quanshengtang was an important base of Guangdong Heaven and Earth Society to secretly train anti-Qing personnel.

In order to train more talents as soon as possible, Chen Jin'gang and Zhu Ziru reformed the training methods taught by Hong Xiguan and Zhu Fu. A new training model with "the Hong Beginning and the Cai Ending" was formed with the bridge hands and horse stances of Hong Quan as the basis and by absorbing the cream of Three-Extension Fist, Three-Wire Falling Iron Fist and Fast Fist of Hong Quan and the fast striking methods of Cai Jia Quan and Fo Jia Quan (Buddhist Family Fist).

Apart from this Hong Quan branch which has been passed down from generation to generation, there is another branch in Sanshui District, which was passed down by Hong Shenggong, a descendant of Hong Xiguan. This branch spread as Hong Shenggong moved from Zhuyaoling, Zhudong Village, Chini Town, Huaxian County to Daozhuang Village, Datang Town, Sanshui, Foshan. Hong Quan of Sanshui District not only features traditional routines like Butterfly Palms, Hong Quan with Six-Point-Five Clubs, Six-Point-Five Clubs, Double-Head Clubs, and Big Rakes, but also the creative routines of "the Hong Beginning and the Cai Ending" which was developed during the wartime, so it is a precious resource in the treasure bank of Lingnan Hong Quan techniques. [1]

VIII. Huang Feihong Lion Dancing and Martial Arts Academy

In 1996, Huang Feihong Lion Dancing and Martial Arts Academy was completed in Huang's hometown, Luzhou Village at the foot of the Xiqiao Mountain, Nanhai District, Foshan City. The academy has been transformed from the Huang Ancestral Hall and has been part of the Xiqiao Mountain Scenic Spot.

The Lion Dancing Team of Huang Feihong Lion Dancing and Martial Arts Academy has won numerous honors.

---

1 Hong Yongqiang. "Origin of Historical Inheritance of 'Quanshengtang's Hong Quan", in the 2nd Volume of *Folks*, by Folk Artists Association of Sanshui District.

会早期的核心人物之一，曾参加陈四（绰号“烂屐四”）于清嘉庆七年（1802）领导的惠州博罗天地会起义。起义失败后回到花县炭步、李溪等地设馆传授洪拳。

陈金釭（1820—1865），本名泽，三水县范湖镇清湖村人。少时家贫，青年时期入朱福所设的“全胜堂”洪拳武馆学艺（武馆后由朱福儿子朱子儒打理）。“全胜堂”表面是武馆，其实为广东天地会的一个重要堂口，秘密训练反清之士。

为了在尽量短的时间内培养有生力量，陈金釭、朱子儒改革了洪熙官、朱福传授洪拳的训练方法，在传统三展拳、三线落铁拳、快拳等套路中选取精华，以洪拳桥马为根基，吸收蔡家拳和佛家拳的快打手法，形成了“洪头蔡尾”的训练模式。

三水区的洪拳除此数代相传的洪拳分支之外，还有一支出自洪熙官的后裔洪胜公，随他从花县赤坭镇竹洞村猪腰岭迁居至三水大塘镇到庄村而流传开来。

三水区的洪拳，既有蝴蝶掌、夹六点半棍洪拳、六点半棍、双头棍、南派缨枪、关刀、双刀、大耙等传统套路，又有战争年代出现的洪拳变式“洪头蔡尾”等创新套路，是岭南洪拳技术宝库中的宝贵资源。[1]

1 洪永强：《洪门“全胜堂”洪家拳传承历史源流》，载三水区民间文艺家协会《民间》第二集。

（八）黄飞鸿狮艺武术馆

1996年，该馆在黄飞鸿家乡佛山市南海区西樵山下的禄舟村建成。它以西樵山风景名胜区为依托，由黄氏宗祠改建而成。

黄飞鸿狮艺武术馆醒狮团曾获诸多殊荣。

（九）佛山黄飞鸿纪念馆

纪念馆坐落在佛山市祖庙博物馆内，2001年1月14日落成并对外开放。

馆内陈列固定，多角度、全方位地展示黄飞鸿作为岭南洪拳一代宗师的典型形象。

除了展示黄飞鸿各方面情况的静态材料之外，每天还有黄飞鸿狮艺武术馆醒狮团展现洪拳和狮艺的精彩动态表演。

黄飞鸿纪念馆已成为佛山重要武术文化窗口。

黄飞鸿纪念馆演武厅
Martial Arts Performing Hall of Huang Feihong Memorial Hall

IX. Foshan Huang Feihong Memorial Hall

Located in Foshan Ancestral Hall Museum, the memorial hall was completed and opened to the public on January 14th, 2001.

The fixed exhibits of the memorial hall display the image of Huang Feihong, a representative master of Lingnan Hong Quan from various angles.

In addition to the static exhibits, there are also wonderful performances of Hong Quan and lion dances by Huang Feihong Martial Arts and Lion Dancing Team every day.

Huang Feihong Memorial Hall has become an important window of Foshan martial arts culture.

2.2 Cai Li Fo Quan

In the late Qing Dynasty, among the five famous Southern martial arts types in Guangdong, Hong Quan still spread and developed while the other four were on the wane. Against this backdrop, Cai Li Fo Quan (Choy Li Fut Fist) emerged as a new martial arts style and was disseminated all over Guangdong Province. Zhang Yan (also known as Cheung Yim) established the Hungsing Gymnasium to cultivate generations of Cai Li Fo Quan masters who, in turn, set up multiple branches not only in Foshan but also in large parts of Jiangmen (including Xinhui, Taishan, Kaiping and Enping), Guangzhou and Hong Kong. Consequently, Cai Li Fo Quan has spread all over the world and exerted strong influences on the development of traditional martial arts.

I. Origin of Cai Li Fo Quan and its introduction into Foshan

Cai Li Fo Quan can be traced back to the ancient Xinhui County in the Qing Dynasty (now the Xinhui District of Jiangmen City, Guangdong Province). It is a prestigious type of Southern martial arts, boasting a distinguished style of techniques, a complete system, widespread dissemination, and profound influences.

There exist two opinions on the founder of Cai Li Fo Quan.

The first is that this martial arts type was established by Chen Xiang born in Gongbeili, Jingmei Village, Yamen Town, Xinhui. In the 16th year of the Daoguang period (1836) of the Qing Dynasty, Chen initiated the Cai Li Fo Quan which kept a balance between offense and defense with a combination of soft and hard techniques of different styles. It was so named to honor Chen's

第二节　蔡李佛拳

清末，广东南拳五大名拳中洪拳尚有传承，其他拳种逐渐式微。而此时蔡李佛拳异军突起，分布于广东各地，尤其是张炎建立的佛山鸿胜馆，培育了一代又一代武林英才。鸿胜馆门徒除在佛山建立众多分馆外，在四邑一带（新会、台山、开平和恩平）及广州、香港等地也设立了多家分馆，传播蔡李佛拳，并辐射至世界各地，对中国传统武术发展影响较大。

佛山鸿胜纪念馆，以始建于清代的太上庙为馆址（何绍鉴供图）
Foshan Hungsing Memorial Hall, located in Taishang Temple built in the Qing Dynasty (photo provided by He Shaojian)

（一）蔡李佛拳溯源与传入佛山

蔡李佛拳发源于古新会县（今广东省江门市新会区），是技术

蔡李佛拳

Cai Li Fo Quan

teachers, namely Cai Fu (Choy Fook), Li Youshan (Li Yau-San), and Chen Yuanhu (Chan Yuen-Wu) whose martial arts were of Buddhist origin. [1]

The other is that Chen Xiang and his student Zhang Yan founded Cai Li Fo Quan together. The martial arts type was established by combining Cai Jia Quan Li Jia Quan, and the Internal and External Bagua Palms which Zhang had learned from Monk Green Grass in the Bapai Mountain of Guangxi. [2]

According to *History of Martial Arts in Guangdong*, in the 29th year of the Daoguang period (1849) of the Qing Dynasty, Chen Xiang built the first Cai Li Fo Ancestral Hall in Xinhui and branch halls all over Guangdong Province. In 1851, Zhang Yan founded the Hungsing Hall in Foshan.

II. Development of Foshan Hungsing Hall

1. Zhang Yan founding the hall and laying a solid foundation

In 1851, the Hungsing Hall founded by Zhang Yan was located in the Huo Clan Ancestral Hall in Mitingtou, Zhaxia, Foshan. Before long, Zhang was involved in the Taiping Rebellion (an uprising to overthrow the Qing Dynasty) and served as a coach in the army. In 1864 when the movement failed, he fled to Hong Kong, and three years later he went back to Foshan to reopen the hall and promote anti-Qing thoughts.

2. Chen Sheng succeeding to develop it

Among all the students of Zhang Yan's, Chen Sheng who had learned Cai Li Fo Quan from him for ten years came out as the most outstanding. Therefore, Chen took the helm after Zhang died from illnesses in 1893.

---

1 Fang Jianhong. *Picture Album of the Intangible Cultural Heritage in Guangdong Province (1).* Guangzhou: World Publishing Guangdong Corporation, 2010, p. 236.

2 This conclusion was drawn based on years of textual research made by Huang Zhenjiang, the head of Foshan Hungsing Hall, and Deng Guangmin, a martial arts scholar, by integrating manuscripts of *A Brief Biography of Zhang Yan* written by Tang Dongchen and *A Biography of Zhang Hungsing* written by Chen Huacan, apprentice of Chen Yaochi who was a grandson of Chen Xiang.

The Hungsing Hall was in its heyday since Chen Sheng' takeover to the mid-1920s.

3. Involvement in Communist movements and thriving in blood and fire

(1) Li Su, a core member of the United League of China

When the Foshan Branch of the United League of China (which was initiated by Dr. Sun Yat-sen to overthrow the Qing Dynasty) was founded in 1912, Li Su, a student of Zhang Yan's, took charge of it. Its members also included Qian Weifang, Wang Hanjin, Feng Jianbo, Feng Ziyou and others.

(2) Qian Weifang, a member of the Communist Party of China (CPC)

In 1921, Qian Weifang and his junior fellow students Liang Guihua and Chen Xiongzhi were admitted to the CPC at the recommendation of Liang Furan. Together, they formed the earliest Party group in Foshan and ushered in the vigorous revolutionary movements for the city.

(3) Liang Guihua, a representative of the Labor Movements

In 1923, the CPC organized the "Group of Ten Communist Laborers" in Foshan, making it the leading nucleus of the labor movements. Liang Guihua was one of the ten members. Under the Group's leadership, economic struggles in various industries succeeded in a row.

(4) Wu Qin, commander of the Peasant Army

Wu Qin was a student of Qian Weifang's. In the autumn of 1923, Liang Furan, Qian Weifang and Liang Guihua were sent by the Foshan Branch of the CPC to contact with Wu, since they all had practiced martial arts in Foshan Hungsing Hall. The three promoted communism to Wu and persuaded him into following the suggestion of the Party, namely, building a peasant armed force. In May 1924, the Nanpu Peasant Army in Foshan was established. Wu, as the commander, was credited with being the pioneer to lead the peasant movements in the Pearl River Delta. The peasant army was also honored to have received Liao Zhongkai, a prominent leader in the Democratic Revolution in China.

4. Hungsing Hall developed into Hungsing Sports Association

In 1937, Hungsing Sports Association was established by Yu Shaofu, Lin Xing, Chen Yilin, and Tang Xi. It had 123 members, with old members of Hungsing Hall and new members each accounting for 50%. The Sports Association,

风格独特、体系完整、流传广泛、影响深远的著名南派拳种。

关于蔡李佛拳的开宗立派者，目前有两种说法。

一是出生于新会崖门镇京梅村拱北里的陈享。清道光十六年（1836），陈享集蔡、李、陈等多家拳法、拳术、腿技之长，独创了刚柔相济、攻防兼备的武术技法，并取其恩师蔡福、李友山的姓氏和另一恩师陈远护的拳术与佛门之渊源而命名为蔡李佛拳[1]。

二是陈享和张炎师徒二人。陈享和张炎将蔡家拳、李家拳和张炎在广西八排山随青草和尚所学的佛门内外八卦掌整合成蔡李佛拳[2]。

《广东武术志》载：陈享于清道光二十九年（1849）在家乡创建蔡李佛祖师堂，并在广东各地设立分馆。张炎从新会到佛山设立鸿胜馆是1851年。

（二）佛山鸿胜馆的发展

1. 张炎创馆，建立根基

1851年，张炎在佛山创办鸿胜馆，最早馆址位于佛山栅下米艇头霍家祠。开馆后不久，张炎即参加太平天国运动，并于军中任教练，后于1864年逃亡至香港，1867年重返佛山复馆，并将反清思想

1　方健宏：《广东省非物质文化遗产名录图典（一）》，广东世界图书出版公司2010年版，第236页。

2　佛山鸿胜馆馆长黄镇江、武术研究学者邓光民等根据多年调查，结合唐栋臣《张炎小传》手稿和陈享之孙陈耀麓的徒弟陈华灿的《张鸿胜传》手稿，考证得此结论。

灌输给弟子。

2. 陈盛继任，光大门楣

在张炎众多弟子中，陈盛的功夫最为了得，他追随张炎学艺10年。1893年，张炎因病去世，鸿胜馆由陈盛执掌。

从陈盛执掌鸿胜馆至20世纪20年代中期，是鸿胜馆蔡李佛拳发展壮大和最辉煌的时期。

3. 红色武馆，血的洗礼

（1）中国同盟会骨干李苏

李苏为张炎弟子，钱维方为陈盛首徒。1912年，佛山成立中国同盟会支部，由李苏负责，会员有钱维方、王寒烬、冯鉴波和冯自由等人。

（2）革命党人钱维方

1921年，梁复燃介绍钱维方、梁桂华、陈雄志加入中国共产党，组成佛山最早的共产党小组。梁桂华、陈雄志为钱维方的师弟。从此，佛山展开轰轰烈烈的革命运动。

（3）工人运动代表梁桂华

1923年，中国共产党在佛山组织了佛山工人“共产主义十人团”（以下简称“十人团”），作为工人运动的领导核心。梁桂华是十人团成员之一。在十人团的领导下，各行业的经济斗争接连取得胜利。

蔡李佛拳
Cai Li Fo Quan

compared with the old Hungsing Hall which solely taught Cai Li Fo Quan, featured more programs, for it contained divisions of martial arts, ball games, entertainment, music and finance.

III. Cai Li Fo Quan spreading overseas

Foshan Hungsing Hall's Cai Li Fo Quan spread overseas during the late Qing Dynasty and the Republic of China. Many who had followed the founder Zhang Yan, established gymnasiums in Hong Kong, Southeast Asia, and even Americas to teach Cai Li Fo Quan.

IV. Freehand fighting and weapon routines of Foshan Cai Li Fo Quan

Current freehand fighting and weapon routines of Cai Li Fo Quan disseminated in Foshan are inherited from the Zhang Yan Sect. When he was at the helm, Chen Sheng, based on years of experience and teaching practices, simplified and reformed the relatively long routines. Later, the successor of Chen further reduced the freehand fighting and weapon routines to facilitate dissemination. In terms of weapon routines, more traditional ones have been preserved.

Hungsing Hall mainly teaches freehand fighting and weapon routines. Members learn level fists, clubs, knock fighting, double broadswords, single broadswords, benches, rakes, single-head clubs, whips, double whips, spears, single broadswords versus shields, double shields, sparring and 23 techniques of Cai Li Fo Quan (such as the Internal and External Bagua Fists).

1. Major freehand fighting routines of Cai Li Fo Quan

A distinguishing feature of Cai Li Fo Quan is the horizontal stance (meaning the height of the stance is relatively low). Major routines include Level Fists, Long Fists, Knock-Fighting Fists, Drunken Fists, Jiazi Fists (which mainly use the legs and feet), Taizi Fists (which mainly use the elbows and knees), War Fists, Buddhist Palms, Cross Pattern Fists, Plum Blossom Fists, Forty-Form Fists, and Southern Stake Fists.

（4）农民军领头人吴勤

吴勤为钱维方的徒弟。1923年秋，中国共产党佛山组织派梁复燃、钱维方、梁桂华等人，以鸿胜馆的旧谊与吴勤交往，以对他进行宣传教育，使吴勤接受了党组织的建议，组织农民武装。1924年5月，佛山南浦乡农团成立。吴勤任团长，成为珠江三角洲领导农民运动的第一人。廖仲恺曾亲临农团指导。

4. 从鸿胜馆到鸿胜体育会

1937年，余少甫、林杏、陈艺林、汤锡等人建立鸿胜体育会，会员123人，原来鸿胜馆的馆员与新加入的会员各占其半。会内设国术部、球类部、游艺部、音乐部、理财部等，与原来鸿胜馆单纯传授蔡李佛拳相比，鸿胜体育会活动项目更为丰富。

（三）蔡李佛拳海外流传

鸿胜馆蔡李佛拳在晚清和民国时期已经传至境外，创始人张炎的传人中，有许多到香港地区和东南亚及美洲一带设馆授徒。

（四）佛山蔡李佛拳拳术及器械套路

佛山目前流传的蔡李佛拳拳术及器械套路是从张炎一脉传承下来的。到陈盛执掌时，他总结多年经验，结合教拳实践，将蔡李佛拳较长的套路简化、改革。后来，佛山鸿胜馆第三代传人又对拳术套路进行了整理，以便推广。器械方面传承下来的传统套路较多。

鸿胜馆以拳术和器械为主科，会员依次学习平拳、棍、扣打拳、双刀、单刀、凳、耙、单头棍、鞭、双鞭、枪、单刀盾牌、双盾、对拆和蔡李佛拳拳法中的23种武艺（如内、外八卦拳）。

1. 蔡李佛拳主要拳术套路

最大特点是所有套路均开横桩，主要有平拳、长拳、扣打拳、醉酒烂打、家字拳、太字拳、战拳、佛掌、十字拳、梅花拳、四十式、南桩拳等。

2. 蔡李佛拳主要器械套路

蔡李佛拳的器械套路，都是在实战中发展起来的。主要有飞鼠扑壁双刀、大刀栏门寨、单刀藤牌碟、枪术、抗日大刀、双夹单棍、棍术、风雷箫、锄头功、板凳功、大耙、三股叉。奇门兵器还有穿云伞、游龙扇等。

（五）佛山蔡李佛拳拳术技术特色

可用4句话概括：腰灵膊活飞砣劲，偏身出手快如风。腾挪闪避进退稳，横标直插腰腿功。

手法：标、撞、挂、扫、插、抛、抡、擒、拨、蟠、截、挑、爪、掌、指、顶、肘等。

步法：四平、弓步、扭、拐、偷、虚、骑、跪等。

腿法：双飞、横钉、旋风、撑虎、穿心、扫堂、铲腿、观音坐莲、罗汉扫地等。

2. Major weapon routines of Cai Li Fo Quan

Weapon routines of the martial arts have evolved in actual fighting.

Major weapon routines include "Flying Mouse Pouncing on the Wall" Double Broadswords, "Gatekeeper" Broadswords, Broadswords versus Rattan Shields, spears, "Anti-Japanese Aggression" Broadswords, Double-Clip Single Clubs, clubs, Tempest Xiao (a vertical bamboo flute), hoes, benches, rakes, and ox horn-shaped tridents; and strange weapons such as Cloud Penetrating Umbrellas and Wandering Dragon Fans.

V. Technical characteristics of Cai Li Fo Quan

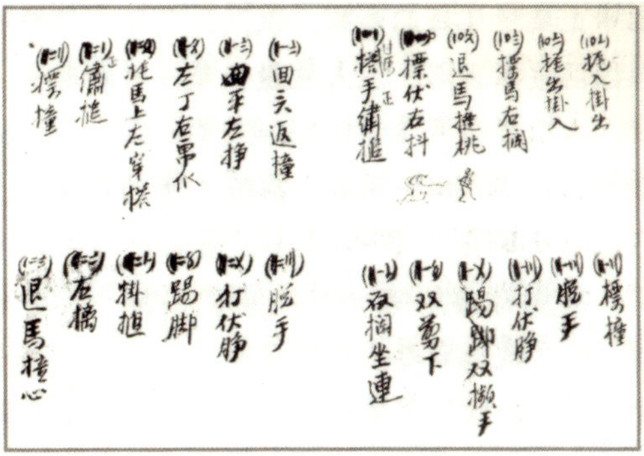

蔡李佛拳拳谱（何绍鉴供图）

Manual of Cai Li Fo Quan (photo provided by He Shaojian)

It could be summarized in four sentences. With a flexible waist, the practitioner moves his arm agilely and powerfully like a flying stone. He fights sideways and attacks swiftly like the wind. He moves and dodges forward and backward stably. He punches forcefully upward and knuckle strikes with strength from his waist and legs combined.

Hand techniques: diagonal upward power shot, small upward power shot, back fist, sweeping, knuckle strike, upward power shot, swinging power shot, pressing palm deflection, pulling out, twisting, blocking, hook punch, clawing, slapping, pointing, pushing, and elbowing.

Footwork: square stance, bow stance, twisting stance, crippling stance, stealing stance, empty stance, riding stance, and kneeling stance.

Leg techniques: double-leg kicking, nailing, whirlwind kicking, bracing, heart-piercing kicking, circular foot sweeping, diagonal downward kicking, Guanyin Sitting on Lotus, and Lohan Sweeping.

VI. Foshan Hungsing Memorial Hall

Foshan Hungsing Memorial Hall is located in Taishang Temple, a cultural relic under municipal protection whose restoration cost over one million RMB financed by the government in 1998.

1. Excavating and sorting out traditional Cai Li Fo Quan

Disciples of Foshan Hungsing Hall have excavated and sorted out over 40 freehand fighting and weapon routines. They taught this martial art not only in Hungsing Hall, Hungsing Liang Hall, and Hungsing School, but also in ordinary schools. As Hungsing Hall emphasizes talent training, more than 70 students have gained national martial arts certificates over the years.

2. Successful inheritance of Cai Li Fo Quan

Foshan Hungsing Hall has taught Cai Li Fo Quan in seven primary schools and one middle school. According to incomplete statistics, more than 10,000 students have learned and practiced it. Consequently, Foshan Hungsing Hall has been credited as a demonstration unit for introducing martial arts into schools by the Sports Bureau and Education Bureau of Foshan.

VII.Successors of Foshan Hungsing Hall

Foshan Hungsing Hall has enjoyed a history of over 160 years and is now listed as an intangible cultural heritage project of Guangdong Province. Apart from the aforementioned representatives, its lineage also includes Huang Si, Zhou Changqing, and 16 other major successors.

（六）佛山鸿胜纪念馆

1998年，政府拨款100多万元，修复市级文物保护单位太上庙，作为佛山鸿胜纪念馆馆址。

1. 发掘整理蔡李佛拳传统套路

佛山鸿胜馆门人发掘整理拳械套路超过40套，除在鸿胜馆、鸿胜梁馆、鸿胜堂教学外，还走进校园开展教学活动。鸿胜馆注重人才培养，历年考取国家武术段位的有70多人。

2. 传承教学显成效

佛山鸿胜馆已经在7所小学和1所中学教授蔡李佛拳。据不完全统计，历年来接受过鸿胜蔡李佛拳拳械训练的学生超过1万人。佛山鸿胜馆被佛山市体育局、佛山市教育局定为武术进校园示范单位。

（七）鸿胜馆内有传人

鸿胜馆在佛山有160多年历史。目前，蔡李佛拳已被列入广东省非物质文化遗产保护项目，其传承谱系除包含上面提到的代表性人物外，还有黄四、周常青等18位主要传人。

第三节　咏春拳

咏春拳是南拳体系中的内家拳种，具有刚柔相济、发力含蓄、后发先至等特征。相传起源于福建南少林寺，清代中后期经粤剧红船弟子传入佛山，从此落地生根，历代繁衍，并以佛山为中心，向广州、鹤山、中山等珠江三角洲城市发展，辐射国内多个省、区、市，进而传播至世界各地，成为世界上最流行的拳种之一。

（一）咏春拳历史溯源

1. 严咏春创拳说

清代中期，福建南少林寺俗家弟子严四之女严咏春在练武期间偶见蛇鹤相争，深受启发，在自己原有武功基础上创编了咏春拳。

2. 五枚师太创拳说

为福建永春白鹤拳高手五枚师太所创。清乾隆二十八年（1763），福建南少林寺被清兵焚毁，五枚师太避祸隐居于川滇边界大凉山，因见蛇鹤争斗而领悟拳理，创出一套独特拳术传给了女弟子严咏春。

2.3 Yongchun Quan

As an internal type of Southern martial arts, Yongchun Quan (Wing Chun Kung Fu)is characterized by its coordination of hardness and softness, controlled movements and late-mover advantages. Legend has it that Yongchun Quan had its root in the Southern Shaolin Temple of Fujian and spread to Foshan by Red Boat Cantonese Opera troupes during the mid and late Qing Dynasty. Since then, Yongchun Quan has taken root and developed in Foshan over the years. Later it spread to Guangzhou, Heshan and Zhongshan with Foshan as the hub. It has gained popularity throughout China and across the world, becoming one of the most popular martial arts types worldwide.

I. Origins of Yongchun Quan

1. Yan Yongchun as the creator

In the mid Qing Dynasty, Yan Yongchun, the daughter of Yan Si, who was a secular disciple at the Southern Shaolin Temple, created this martial arts type on the basis of the martial arts she had learned earlier and the inspiration she had gained from the fight between a snake and a crane.

2. Buddhist Nun Wumei (or Ng Mui) as the creator

It is said that it was created by Buddhist Nun Wumei, a master of White Crane Fist in Yongchun, Fujian. In the 28th year of the Qianlong period (1763) of the Qing Dynasty, after the Fujian Southern Shaolin Temple was burned down by the Qing army, Wumei fled to Daliangshan on the border of Sichuan and Yunnan provinces. During her stay there, she synthesized a set of unique martial arts after being inspired by a fight between a snake and a crane and then imparted it to her female disciple Yan Yongchun.

3. Abbess Yichen as the creator

Yichen, the abbess of Songshan Shaolin Temple and a member of the anti-Qing Heaven and Earth Society, assimilated all that she had studied over the years to create Yongchun Quan.

4. Zen Master Zhishan as the disseminator

According to another legend, Yongchun Quan was named after the Yong Chun Hall in Southern Shaolin Temple in Quanzhou, Fujian Province. Its full name was "Shaolin Yongchun Quan". Zen Master Zhishan who was good at it taught it in the temple.

5. Hu Huiqian as the disseminator

Hu Huiqian born in Xinhui, Guangdong, was a friend of Fang Shiyu's (Fang was a Chinese martial arts master and folk hero in Guangdong in the Qing Dynasty). Hu went to Southern Shaolin Temple to learn martial arts in hope of seeking revenge for his father, who ran a small shop in the vicinity of Jinlun Guild Hall in Xiguan, Guangzhou and was beaten to death by villains. During his stay in the Temple, Hu acquired Yongchun Quan and Hua Quan (Flower Fist).

Most followers believe that Southern Shaolin Temple is the cradle of Yongchun Quan which features snake-like or crane-like hand movements. It was introduced into Foshan in the mid-Qing Dynasty and had close relationships with anti-Qing organizations and Red Boat Cantonese Opera troupes.

II. Major inheritors of Foshan Yongchun Quan

The major inhertiors of Foshan Yongchun Quan can be divided into five major sects according to their origins.

1. The First Major Sect

The first and the largest sect among all, was passed on by Shaolin disciple Liang Fuchou to Huang Huabao and Liang Erdi, both of whom were local opera artists in Foshan. But it was also said that Liang Erdi learned martial arts from Zen

咏春拳
Yongchun Quan

3. 一尘庵主创拳说

清代初年，反清组织“天地会”中的嵩山少林弟子一尘庵主，融合多年武学心得创出咏春拳。

4. 至善禅师传拳说

咏春拳原名永春拳，因福建泉州南少林寺永春殿而得名，是南少林内家拳法，全称“少林永春拳”。至善禅师擅长此拳，在寺中教习。

5. 胡惠乾传拳说

方世玉之友、广东新会人胡惠乾，其父在广州西关锦纶堂附近开设小商店，被机房恶汉殴毙。他为报父仇到南少林寺学艺，在永春殿内学得咏春拳和花拳。

大部分传人认为咏春拳源自福建南少林寺。咏春拳手法以蛇、鹤形态为特色，清代中期传入佛山，与反清组织和红船戏班有密切关系。

（二）佛山咏春拳主要传承脉络

佛山咏春拳有众多传人，溯其宗源，可分为5条主线。

1. 第一主线

这是佛山咏春拳最大的传承支系，由少林弟子梁傅俦传给佛山本地戏班艺人黄华宝和梁二娣（也有说梁二娣的功夫是由至善禅师所传），二人又传武于梁赞。目前佛山90%以上咏春拳的支脉为梁赞的传人，佛山咏春拳传人普遍认为梁赞是佛山咏春拳第

Master Zhishan. Later Huang and Liang passed on Yongchun Quan to Liang Zan who was believed to be the first-generation master of Foshan Yongchun Quan since more than 90% of its practitioners in Foshan are his successors.

梁赞真像（佛山市博物馆藏）

Portrait of Liang Zan (stored in Foshan Museum)

2. The Second Major Sect

Luo Wan'gong passed on Yongchun Quan to Guo Baoquan from Qinzhou, Guangxi, and Guo imparted it to Ruan Jiyun, a native of Foshan in the late Qing Dynasty.

3. The Third Major Sect

Lu Wu passed Yongchun Quan on to Lu Biao, who then passed it on to Lu Jin, a local opera artists in Foshan who later became the first-generation master of this sect.

4. The Fourth Major Sect

Yi Jin, passed it on to Cao Yinsheng and Cao Shunhe. This sect is also called "Yahu Yongchun".

5. The Fifth Major Sect

Xie Guozhang and Xie Guoliang were the first-generation successors of this sect.

III. The naming of Yongchun

In Chinese, there are three different written forms of Yongchun, namely " 咏春 ", " 詠春 " and " 永春 ". Practitioners explained that " 咏春 " and " 詠春 " conveyed the same meaning for " 詠 " was the traditional character form while " 咏 " was the simplified one that was adopted as a result of the promotion of simplified Chinese in the 1980s. At that time, only the simplified form was available in computers and therefore " 詠春 " was replaced by " 咏春 ". As for " 永春 ", it was more complicated to explain and according to Zhao Licheng (who is a Yongchun inheritor and a daughter of Zhao Jin's, a Yongchun Master in the late Qing Dynasty and the Republic of China), " 永春拳 " was the original name of " 咏春拳 ".

The same martial art has been called by the three different names in different times with different focuses.

IV. Great Foshan Yongchun Masters

1. Great Yongchun masters in the Qing Dynasty

There were Zhang Wu, Liang Fuchou, Liang Lan'gui, Lu Jin, Gao Laozhong, Huang Huabao, Liang Erdi, Liang Zan, Feng Shaoqing and Chen Huashun.

2. Great Yongchun masters in the late Qing Dynasty and the Republic of China

There were Lei Ruji, Wu Zhongsu, Ruan Jiyun, Ruan Qishan, Chen Rujin, Zhao Jiu, Yao Cai, Yip Man and Li Yechi.

3. Great contemporary Yongchun masters

There are Zhang Bao, Peng Nan, Yao Qi, Ye Zhun, and Cen Neng.

V. Technical features of Yongchun Quan

As a practical type of Southern martial arts, Yongchun Quan is highly philosophical and has distinctive regional characteristics, with quick fists, short knives, long poles and close-range combat as its techniques. Many of its skills reflect the profound and practical traditional Chinese philosophy, such as short bridge hands, narrow horse stances, nimble movements, late-mover advantages, the clever use of the opponent's force to fight back, the defeat of force with tenderness, and the use of *Cun Jin* (a kind of internal force with short, clear, and explosive power) as the centerline for defense and counterattack.

1. Major hand movements, footwork and horse stances

Hand movements: There are three major hand movements of Yongchun Quan, namely *Tanshou* (dispersing hands), *Bangshou* (binding hands) and *Fushou* (controlling hands), supplemented with many other hand movements. All these stress the flexibility of the wrists and the strength of the elbows, highlighting the use of opposing forces to change the direction of the opponent's force, making close-range attacks with *Cun Jin* to attack the opponent's shoulder pits, elbows,

一代宗师。

2. 第二主线

由罗晚恭传给广西钦州人郭保全，郭保全于晚清时期传授给佛山人阮济云。

3. 第三主线

由卢五传给陆标，再由陆标传给佛山戏班艺人陆锦（“大花面锦”）。陆锦是该主线第一代宗师。

4. 第四主线

由易金（“白面炳”）传给曹隐胜和曹顺和，别称“雅湖永春”。

5.第五主线

谢国璋、谢国良为该主线第一代传人。

（三）“咏春”“詠春”“永春”的称谓

众咏春师傅解释：“咏春”和“詠春”实质相同，“詠”是繁体字，传统手写抄本均用“詠春”；“咏春”写法出现于20世纪80年代，由于推行简体汉字，当时的计算机字库中只能输入“咏”字，于是出现了两种写法。至于“永春拳”的称谓则稍微复杂一些，据招丽澄（为清末至民国期间的咏春拳名师招就之女，亦为咏春传人）解释，咏春拳原名永春拳。

三种称谓应是同一拳种在不同时期的不同称谓，不存在本质上的不同。

（四）佛山咏春拳名师录

1. 清代咏春拳名师

有张五、梁傅俦、梁兰桂、陆锦、高佬忠、黄华宝、梁二娣、梁赞、冯少青、陈华顺等。

2. 清末至民国期间的咏春拳名师

有雷汝济、吴仲素、阮济云、阮奇山、陈汝棉、招就、姚才、叶问、黎叶篪等。

3. 咏春拳当代名师

有张保、彭南、姚祺、叶准、岑能等。

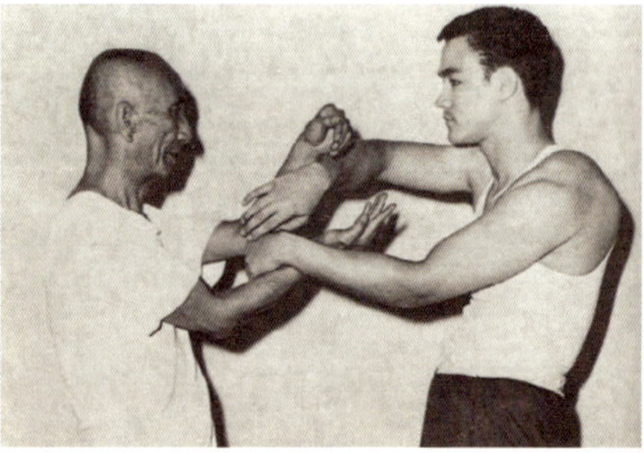

叶问与李小龙演练咏春黐手（照片来自佛山市博物馆）

Yip Man and Bruce Lee practiced Yongchun *Chi Shou* (photo from Foshan Museum)

（五）咏春拳技术特色

咏春拳是一种地域特色鲜明，哲学思想丰富，集快拳、短刀、长棍和近打于一身的南派实用武术。咏春拳短桥窄马，招式灵活，后发先至，借力打力，以柔制刚，以最短的距离和最快的速度，运用“寸劲”于中线防守和借势反击，其招式、套路处处体现深邃、实用的中国传统哲学思想。

lower palms and fingertips.

Footwork: Major footwork includes straight kicks, sideward kicks and upward kicks, all of which attack with heel kicks. When combined in different ways, they form the "Yongchun Eight Feet" in Wooden Dummy Training, which target at the opponent's waist, knees and shins.

Horse stances: Short bridge hands and narrow horse stances are practiced. Erzi Qianyangma, a basic stance of Yongchun, with the feet standing shoulder-width apart, the two legs bending slightly and the knees clamping inward with one-fist width in between, is used in training while Ziwu horse, turning horse, circling horse, thrusting horse, and triangular horse are employed in combat. In close-range combat and *Chi Shou* practice, practitioners are supposed to maintain the centerline, changing the Shaolin front-bow-and-back-arrow stance into the waist bridge horse to approach the opponent as close as possible to offset the opponent's advantage of a wide horse stance.

2. Yongchun *Chi Shou*

Chi Shou, literally meaning "sticky hands", is an exclusive drill of Yongchun Quan. Practiced in a reciprocal manner by following each other's arms back and forth as if you are stuck to the opponent, *Chi Shou* generates thrust in circular and linear motions. One may utilize the opponent's force to fight back against him; contain the opponent when he attacks and launch attacks when he tries to pull back; punch the opponent when his hands have no contact with you; and launch attacks while sensing the opponent's weak points.

VI. Major routines of Yongchun Quan

1. Freehand fighting routines

Major freehand fighting routines of Yongchun Quan include *Xiao Niantou*, *Xun Qiao* and *Biaozhi*.

(1) *Xiao Niantou*, also called *Xiao Liantou*, means "little ideas".

In this form of training, the arms are engaged in repeated linear or circular movements controlled by the mind. Such movements can be explained by the mechanics of machinery in that the upper arms are considered as the cranks

咏春拳

Yongchun Quan

1. 主要手法、脚法和马步

手法：以摊手、绑手、伏手三式为主，辅以枕、窒、圈、弹、拦、径、捆、托、攤、拍、问、标、笈、冲等配套手法，强调腕部的灵巧与肘底的力量，以反作用力顺势改变对手力向，以“寸劲”短距离发力，集中攻击对方的肩窝、肘拐、掌根和指尖。

脚法：以直踢、横撑、上蹬为主，皆以脚跟踢击。这些脚法经过组合，在木人桩法中成“咏春八脚”，直取对方腰、膝、胫等重要部位。

马步：使用短桥窄马。练习时用二字钳阳马，实战时用子午马、转马、圈马、标马、三角马等。在黐手练习或近体搏击中，严守中线，变少林前弓后箭为腰桥马，以方便尽量贴近对方身体，抵消对方长桥大马的优势。

2. 咏春拳黐手

黐手是咏春拳独特的练习形式，由双方的4条臂膀循环往复地相互黏贴翻滚，给力借力，来留去送，甩手直冲，在圆弧和直线运动中形成前推力。

（六）咏春拳主要套路

1. 拳术套路

主要徒手套路有小念头、寻桥和标指等3套拳。

（1）小念头，又叫“小练头”

如用机械力学的原理解释人体运动链，后臂如曲柄，前臂如连杆，则小念头指由人的意念推动进行往复直线移动或圆周转动。

（2）寻桥，是简单直接的击打技术

“桥”是桥手，两个人的手的接触好比一条桥梁把两者连在一起。所谓寻桥，并不是盲目追摸或挡隔对方的手，而是在桥手相接时做出判断和反应，确定对方攻击的来势，从而做出相应的防御动作。

（3）标指，是咏春拳术的高级套路

练习标指旨在学会发力。标指的动作能引导练习者将身体的力在瞬间集中爆发出来，达到力贯指尖的境界。

2. 器械套路

主要器械套路有八斩刀、六点半棍法和木人桩法3种。

（1）八斩刀

咏春拳的短武器，与一般南派短刀相似，双手各执一柄刀，以拦腰、斩脚为绝。

（2）六点半棍法

咏春拳的长武器，与八斩刀一短一长，因应不同场合的需要而使用。六点半棍为单头长棍，全棍长七尺二寸（2.4米），以榕树气根削制为最好。六点半棍打练讲求地盘、腰身、肘、手、腕的和合。

（3）木人桩法

咏春拳训练器械之一。咏春拳的木人桩法从108式到158式不等，各师门依其传授方式略有出入。

佛山现存较早的木人桩谱，是20世纪50年代由叶问弟子汤继整理抄录的手稿，可谓硕果仅存。

while the forearms as the connecting rods.

(2) *Xun Qiao*, meaning "seeking the bridge", is a direct and simple punching technique.

A "bridge" is formed when the practitioners' hands touch each other. Seeking the bridge means making quick decisions and responses to defend oneself by seeking the opponent's attacking trajectory rather than blindly seeking or blocking the opponent's hands.

(3) *Biao Zhi*, meaning darting fingers, is an advanced routine of Yongchun Quan.

The purpose of practicing *Biao Zhi* is to learn how to use one's power. Movements of *Biao Zhi* can guide practitioners to have eruptive power of the body to the extent that even the fingertips are full of strength.

2. Weapon routines

Major weapon routines include Eight Cutting Broadswords, Six-Point-Five Clubs and Wooden Dummy Training.

(1) Eight Cutting Broadsword

It is a short weapon similar to the short knife in Southern martial arts. The practitioner holds two broadswords with one in each hand, targeting at the opponent's waist and feet.

彭南演示咏春木人桩法（彭树藻供图）

Peng Nan demonstrating Wooden Dummy Training of Yongchun (photo provided by Peng Shuzao)

(2) Six-Point-Five Club

Being a long weapon, it is used for purposes different from those of the short weapon of the Eight Cutting Broadsword. It is a single-head pole of 2.4 meters long, the best material of which is the root of banyan trees. When this weapon is used, coordination and harmony of one's sphere of influence, waist, elbows, and wrists are important.

(3) Wooden Dummy Training

It is one of the weapons used in drills. The numbers of movements in Wooden Dummy Training vary in different sects of Yongchun, usually between 108 and 158. The oldest existing manuscript of Foshan Yongchun Wooden Dummy Training is the one collected and sorted out by Tang Ji, a student of Yip Man's in the 1950s.

VII. Philosophy of Yongchun Quan

The following pithy formulas of Yongchun Quan are from Tang Ji's manuscript, provided by Tang Yongzhi.

1. Contain the opponent when he attacks, launch an attack when he tries to pull back and punch him when his hands have no contact with you.
2. Mobilize your elbows when your wrists are contained and vice versa, and use your upper arms when your forearms are contained.
3. Stick to frontal confrontation.
4. Do not use brute force.
5. Attack the opponent when he is in disorder and he who is in disorder ends up being defeated.

VIII. Dissemination and development of Yongchun Quan

In the late Qing Dynasty, Yongchun Quan was disseminated to Vietnam by Ruan Jiyun. Later on, with the labor export, it gained popularity among overseas Chinese around the globe. In recent decades, students of notable masters such as Cen Neng, Yip Man and Peng Nan have opened gymnasiums overseas to teach Yongchun Quan.

Since 1948, Cen Neng's students in Guangzhou have spread to dozens of countries and regions around the world.

Since 1950, there have emerged a large number of Yongchun masters, such as Yip Man and his overseas students including Liang Xiang, Huang Chunliang, Zhao Yun, Huang Guoyou, Gu Sheng, Mei Yi, Bruce Lee, Ye Zhun, Ye Zheng and Yao Zhongqiang, who have been influential at home and abroad.

Apart from giving lessons of Yongchun Quan to lots of exchange students from various countries in Hong Kong, Yip Man was also the teacher of an international kung fu star—Bruce Lee.

（七）咏春拳理

咏春拳技法口诀存于20世纪50年代的汤继手抄本中（由汤永枝提供）。

1. 来留去送，甩手直冲。
2. 擒尾屼头，擒头屼尾，擒中间剽绑起。
3. 鼻对鼻，无往不利。
4. 不斗力。
5. 失形则打，失形者败。

（八）咏春拳的传播与发展

咏春拳清末始由阮济云带到越南，随后在不断的劳工输出过程中被推广到海外华人社会。近几十年间，岑能、叶问、彭南等人的弟子陆续设馆海外。

1948年后，岑能在广州传下的弟子遍布世界数十个国家和地区。

1950年后，咏春拳拥有叶问及其海外弟子梁相、黄淳梁、招允、黄国有、古生、梅逸、李小龙、叶准、叶正、姚忠强等一批知名拳师，在海内外具有较大影响。

叶问除在香港培养了大批各国籍留学生外，还造就了蜚声国际的功夫巨星李小龙。

FOSHAN, CHINA

第三章

民国时期涌现的拳种和武术组织

Chapter 3

Martial Arts Types and Organizations during the Republic of China

在西方近代体育传入中国之前，中华民族已拥有一大批基础深厚的民族传统体育项目和几千年的传统体育文化。

在新时代下，精武体育会在新文化运动中开始向全国发展。除精武体育会之外，民国时期佛山还有南家拳、太极拳、鹰爪拳、螳螂拳、六合八法拳、周家拳等拳种和相应组织，亦各有所长，共同形成佛山民国武术的繁盛局面。

Before modern Western sports were introduced into China, the Chinese nation had had a large number of traditional sports and several thousand years of traditional sports culture.

In the new era, Jingwu sports associations began to develop nationwide during the New Culture Movement. Apart from them, there were also Nan Jia Quan, Taiji Quan, Eagle Claw Fist, Mantis Fist, Six-Harmony and Eight-Method Fist, Zhou Jia Quan, and related organizations in Foshan during the Republic of China, each having its distinctive strengths. All these contributed to the prosperity of martial arts in Foshan in that period.

3.1 Foshan Jingwu Sports Association

I. Establishment and development of Shanghai Jingwu Sports Association

1. Huo Yuanjia accepting a challenge from Hercules O'brien

One day in mid-June 1909, Tianjin martial arts master Huo Yuanjia accepted a challenge to fight with O'brien, a foreigner of unusual strength, who, frightened by Huo's reputation, did not show up at all.

Huo Yuanjia, also called Huo Junqing, was from Xiaonanhe Village in the western suburb (now Xiqing District) of Tianjin. His ancestors made a living as armed escorts. With a solid foundation of martial arts in the family, Huo was a master in the field.

2. From Jingwu Gymnastics Association to Jingwu Sports Association

On July 7th, 1909, China Gymnastics Association with Nong Jinsun as the president and Huo Yuanjia responsible for overseeing the teaching of martial arts and the studying of military knowledge, was established in the former Zhabei District, Shanghai, making it the first non-governmental sports organization in China. The first batch of students included Chen Gongzhe and others. After Huo Yuanjia was killed, in March 1910, China Jingwu Gymnastics Association was relocated and renamed China

精武体育会创始人霍元甲
Huo Yuanjia, the founder of Jingwu Sports Association

第一节　佛山精武体育会

（一）上海精武体育会的创立与发展

1. 霍元甲应战大力士奥皮音

1909年6月中旬某日，天津拳师霍元甲应战洋人大力士奥皮音，而对方慑于其威名，未出战。

霍元甲，字俊卿，天津西郊（今天津市西青区）小南河村人。祖辈以走镖为业，家传武学根基深厚，是技击高手。

2. 从精武体操会到精武体育会

1909年7月7日，由农劲荪任会长、霍元甲主持精武技击和军事研习活动的中国精武体操会在上海原闸北区正式成立，为我国第一个民间体育团体。第一批学员有陈公哲等。霍元甲被害去世后，1910年3月，中国精武体操会迁址，更名为“中国精武体育会”，简称“精武会”，续霍元甲遗志，重振精武事业。

3. 厘定宗旨，倡导现代体育

精武会习武的宗旨为“以技击为根本，以武德为皈依，辅以有益之学科，以最科学之方法整理拳经”，注重发扬尚武精神。以

精武体育会
Jingwu Sports Association

Jingwu Sports Association, and Jingwu Association for short. The Association aimed to carry on Huo's unaccomplished ambition and to rejuvenate martial arts.

3. Determining the purposes and advocating modern sports

The Jingwu Association aimed at "practicing martial arts by relying on martial ethics and useful disciplines and sorting out martial arts classics with the most scientific methods" so as to carry forward the martial spirit. The Jingwu spirit was "patriotism, self-cultivation, justice and helping others". Taking moral, intellectual and physical education as its teaching objectives, it tried to train people with the Jingwu spirit.

4. Numerous great masters to develop new styles of martial arts

The Jingwu Association invited famous martial arts masters from the Yellow River, the Yangtze River and the Pearl River valleys, including Zhao Lianhe, Zhang Fuyou, Huo yuanqing, Chen Weixian, Sun Yufeng, Luo Guangyu, Huo Dongge, Chen Zizheng, and Wu Jianquan, to teach martial arts so that unprecedented new styles took shape.

5. Jingwu enjoying great reputation with arts and arms

Jingwu Association was not only a social or sports association, but also a public welfare school. Apart from martial arts, it was also engaged in culture, medicine and art and offered activities of calligraphy, painting, Mandarin Chinese, photography, Cantonese music, bronze music, string music, Peking Opera, puppet shows, dance, medicine, tourism and debate, which gradually gained popularity among the people.

II. Southward spread and development of Jingwu martial arts

After 1916, Shanghai Jingwu Association started establishing branches in other parts of Shanghai and in nearby cities.

1. The "Five Envoys of Jingwu" going south

In the southward spread and development of Jingwu Association, the "Five Envoys of Jingwu", namely, Chen Gongzhe, Luo Xiao'ao, Chen Shichao, Ye Shutian and Li Huisheng played a vital role.

2. Establishment of Guangdong Jingwu Sports Association

On April 9th, 1919, Guangdong Jingwu Sports Association was established, and a grand inauguration meeting was held at Guangzhou Haizhu Theater.

III. Foshan Jingwu Sports Association

1. Origin of Foshan Jingwu Sports Association

On July 6th, 1921, Foshan Jingwu Preparatory Committee established Foshan Jingwu Sports Association ("Foshan Jingwu Association" for short), which was temporarily located on No. 5 Fenshui West Street. There were 41 initiators and supporters from the sectors of industry and commerce, medicine and pharmaceutics, and education.

2. The organizational structure of Foshan Jingwu Association

It was divided into divisions of general affairs, national gymnastics, arts and entertainment, and cultural affairs.

3. Jingwu martial arts entering schools

After its establishment, in order to publicize the purposes of saving the nation with sports and to popularize Jingwu national gymnastics, Foshan Jingwu Association also taught martial arts in various public and private schools apart from within the organization.

4. Martial arts and coaches in Foshan Jingwu Association

The Southern and Northern martial arts styles congregated at Foshan Jingwu Association were divided into the three schools of the Yellow River, the Yangtze River and the Pearl River valleys. The ten basic sets of Jingwu martial arts all originated from the Yellow River school. The skills of the coaches and the duration of their teaching in Foshan all had direct influences on the inheritance of the Northern martial arts in the city.

5. Subordinate societies under Foshan Jingwu Association

In order to enhance martial arts training, the Association also established a number of societies, including the athlete team, the volunteer team, the model team, the youth team, the mutual encouragement team, the diligence team, the disciplinary team and the service team.

“爱国、修身、正义、助人”为精武精神，以德、智、体三育为教学宗旨，培养与造就精武式的时代新人。

4. 名师汇聚，发扬武术新风

精武会先后聘请了黄河、长江、珠江流域的各派武术名家，包括赵连和、张富猷、霍元卿、陈维贤、孙玉峰、罗光玉、霍东阁、陈子正、吴鉴泉等前来传授武艺，形成了前所未有的武术新风尚。

5. 乃武乃文，精武威名远播

精武会既是一个社会团体，也是一所公益学校，其内涵远远超出了一个体育团体。除武术外，所涉领域还包括文化、医学、艺术等。有临池（书法）、图画、国语、摄影、粤乐、铜乐、弦乐、京剧，还有影戏、舞艺、旅游、雄辩等活动，逐渐深入民心。

（二）精武武术南传发展

1916年后，上海精武会开始在上海各地及附近城市建立分会。

1. “精武五使”南下

在精武会的南传发展中，被称为“精武五使”的陈公哲、罗啸敖、陈士超、叶书田和黎惠生功不可没。

2. 广东精武体育会的创办

广东精武体育会于1919年4月9日成立，并在广州海珠戏院隆重举行成立大会。

（三）佛山精武体育会

1. 佛山精武体育会缘起

1921年7月6日，佛山精武筹备会借址汾水西街5号成立佛山精武体育会（简称“佛山精武会”）。发起及赞成者有工商界、医药界和教育界人士共41人。

2. 佛山精武会组织机构

分为总务部、国操部、游艺部、文事部。

3. 精武国术操进校园

佛山精武会创办后，为宣传体育救国宗旨，普及精武国术操，把武术的传播延伸到了学校。教员除在本会授课外，还分赴市内各所学校或私塾传授武术。

4. 佛山精武会武术与教员

汇集于佛山精武会的南北拳种有黄河、长江、珠江三大流域派系，精武十套基本拳械均源出黄河流域派系。教员本身的技艺及其在佛山教授的时间长短，对于其所属派系拳术在佛山的传承产生了直接的影响。

5. 佛山精武会中的小团体

佛山精武会组织了健儿团、英志团、模范团、童子团、共勉团、精勤团、策勤团、服务团等，都是为加强武术训练而建立的。

6. 佛山精武会文事和游艺

（1）黄少强与“精社”

黄少强是岭南画派大师高奇峰的入室弟子。他曾是佛山精武会

6. Cultural affairs, arts and entertainment of Foshan Jingwu Association

(1) Huang Shaoqiang and the Jing Society

Huang Shaoqiang was a formal student of Gao Qifeng, a great master of Lingnan-style painting. Huang was a key figure in Foshan Jingwu Association. He established the Jing Society under the Jingwu Association and created a number of paintings on the theme of Jingwu.

(2) Jingwu publicity meetings and the Debating Division

Since 1923, Foshan Jingwu Association held publicity meetings twice or thrice each year to publicize the purposes of the Association and to offer its members a platform to demonstrate their martial arts skills. This not only encouraged them to speak in public, but also cultivated more talented public speakers. In 1924, Li Peixian and Lu Zhiwen established the Debating Division and organized several dozen members to participate in public speaking and debating.

1922年位于莲花地的佛山精武会第一会址
The first location of Foshan Jingwu Association at Lianhuadi in 1922

(3) Characteristic Jingwu dances

There were mainly 13 types of dances, including funny dance, martial arts dance, health dance, phoenix dance, shield dance, Zhuang dance, butterfly dance, pair dance, star dance, sword dance, republic dance, peace dance and Bodhi dance.

(4) Cantonese music and opera of Jingwu Association

Between the mid-1920s and the eve of the War of Resistance against Japanese Aggression, music and operas played an important role in the publicity and entertainment activities of Foshan Jingwu Association each year. Alternating with martial arts

精武体育会

Jingwu Sports Association

的中坚人物，在精武会中创办过“精社”，创作过一批以精武为题材的画作。

（2）精武宣讲会与雄辩部

1923年后，佛山精武会每年都会举办两三次大型宣讲会，旨在扩大宣传精武会的办会宗旨，引起社会关注，同时为会员提供一个展示武术技艺的平台。这训练了会员上台宣讲的勇气，培养出很多演说人才。1924年，李佩弦和陆志文发起成立雄辩部，组织数十名会员参与演说和辩论。

（3）独具特色的精武舞蹈

主要有滑稽舞、武化舞、健康舞、凤舞、盾舞、庄舞、蝶舞、对舞、星舞、剑舞、共和舞、和平舞、菩提舞13种舞蹈。

（4）精武会的粤乐与戏剧

从20世纪20年代中期到抗日战争以前，佛山精武会所组织的历次宣讲和游艺活动中，曲艺和戏剧都是重头戏，常与国操项目穿插表演，深受民众欢迎。精武会的曲艺和戏剧活动之所以繁荣活跃，与佛山肥沃的民间艺术土壤和精武会“以武术为龙头，辅以有益之学科”的办会理念有着密不可分的关系。

（5）期刊出版

佛山精武会于1925年夏创办《佛山精武月刊》（梁敦远、萧剑农赞助），其宗旨是“宣传精武主义，提倡各种科学，借文字、美术赞助人群社会”。《佛山精武月刊》出版20余期后停办。其后，曾有王少波、黄国光编辑《佛山精武周刊》。

（四）由佛山组创的广西梧州精武会

在佛山精武会成立后的第五年，广西梧州精武会成立。梧州精武会的创建，与佛山有莫大的关系。梧州是当时广西繁盛的都会之一，也是中国南部的重要商埠，两广之间商贸往来十分频繁。其时，何心平既是佛山某银号经理，也是精武会的一名骨干。1925年夏，他因商务寓居梧州九坊街卫元银号，与当地商人严方伯、梁杞侪等在商谈之余，积极宣扬精武宗旨。严、梁二位爱国商人也认同当时情势“非讲究国操武术不足以补偏救国”，于是积极邀集各界人士参与筹组。1925年9月11日，梧州精武会筹备会议在梧州同园挹翠楼召开。

（五）中山公园内佛山精武会的筹建过程

建设佛山精武新会所的用地从申请到核批只短短数月，这不但体现了佛山精武会骨干的办事能力，也说明了当时南海县政府在发展民众体育事业方面还是相当开明的。

performances, they enjoyed great popularity among the audience. The Jingwu music and operas had flourished, which was closely related to Foshan's rich folk art tradition and the Association's educational philosophy of making martial arts the locomotive with the support of useful disciplines.

(5) Publication of journals

In the summer of 1925, Foshan Jingwu Association founded *Foshan Jingwu Monthly*, which was sponsored by Liang Dunyuan and Xiao Jiannong. It aimed to "publicize the Jingwu spirit, advocate various sciences and sponsor people and society with words and fine arts". The publication of *Foshan Jingwu Monthly* stopped after over 20 issues. Later, Wang Shaobo and Huang Guoguang published *Foshan Jingwu Weekly* for some time.

IV. Guangxi Wuzhou Jingwu Association created by Foshan

In the fifth year after the establishment of Foshan Jingwu Association, Guangxi Wuzhou Jingwu Association was founded, which was closely related to Foshan. Wuzhou was one of the most flourishing cities in Guangxi and an important commercial port in southern China, with frequent commercial and trade exchanges between Guangxi and Guangdong. At that time, He Xinping was not only the manager of a private bank in Foshan but also a backbone of the Jingwu Association. In the summer of 1925, he lived at Weiyuan Bank on Jiufang Street in Wuzhou on business. While discussing business affairs with the local businessmen such as Yan Fangbo and Liang Qichai, he also advocated the Jingwu spirit. Yan and Liang, the two patriotic businessmen, sharing with him the view about the social situation, maintaining that "only martial arts can save the country", invited people from different sectors to establish Wuzhou Jingwu Assoction. On September 11th, 1925, the Preparatory Meeting was held at Yicui Tower in Wuzhou.

V. The development of Foshan Jingwu Association in Sun Yat-sen Park

It took only several months between the application for and approval of the new site of Foshan Jingwu Association. This not only reflected the strong abilities of the backbones of Foshan Jingwu Association, but also the open-mindedness of the then Nanhai Government in developing public sports.

In 1935, the auditorium was completed. Seeing that the goal was about to be realized, Liang Dunyuan, the President of Foshan Jingwu Association, alone donated money to build the west building and converted it into the Jingwu Martial Arts Academy. Completed in 1936, the Academy started enrolling students and employed Lu Weichang from Shanghai Jingwu Sports Association as its honorary president. The Academy later became an important base for martial arts training in Foshan.

VI. Jingwu schools and enterprises

1. Schools created by Foshan Jingwu Association

Foshan Jingwu Association was the first non-governmental sports association to run schools during the Republic of China, contributing a lot to Foshan's education. Altogether it had established four schools, namely, Taojie Girls' School, Yuanjia School, Yuanjia Folk School, and Jingwu Martial Arts Academy.

2. Yuanjia Soy Sauce Workshop and Yuanjia Industrial Society

In order to make its endeavors sustainable, Foshan Jingwu Association was active in running Jingwu enterprises.

In 1928, Liang Dunyuan, He Xinping and Lu Zhiwen jointly raised funds to establish Yuanjia Soy Sauce Workshop and Lyu Zihe and He Xinping were responsible for organizing the development of Yuanjia Soy Sauce. The workshop was the first one to use modern technology to brew soy sauce in Foshan in the 1930s. Foshan Jingwu Association also established Yuanjia Industrial Society to deal in stationery and paper to finance the development of the Association.

3. Foshan Jingwu Association during the War of Resistance against Japanese Aggression

In 1937, the War of Resistance against Japanese Aggression broke out in full scale and in October the next year, Foshan was occupied. The Jingwu Association was also victimized and the site was used by the Japanese army as a granary. The

1935年，大礼堂落成。眼见目标克日可成，佛山精武会董事长梁敦远为善不甘人后，独资捐建西座用作精武国术学院。1936年，精武国术学院落成后开班授课，聘请上海精武体育会卢炜昌任名誉院长。精武国术学院成为佛山武术培训的重要基地。

（六）精武办学与实业

1. 佛山精武会创办的学校

佛山精武会开创了民国时期佛山民间体育社团办学之先河，为佛山教育事业贡献良多。创办的学校有4所：陶洁女校、元甲学校、元甲平民义学、精武国术学院。

2. 元甲豉油坊与元甲工业社

佛山精武会为使事业可持续发展，积极创办精武实业。

1928年，梁敦远与何心平、陆志文等共同筹资，创办元甲豉油坊，由吕子和、何心平负责组织研制元甲豉油。元甲豉油坊是20世纪30年代佛山最早运用先进生产技术酿制豉油的作坊。佛山精武会还在福禄路开设元甲工业社经营文具、纸张等用品，以实业经费支持会务发展。

3. 抗日战争时期的佛山精武会

1937年，抗日战争全面爆发，次年10月佛山沦陷。精武会未能幸免于难，会址被日军占作粮仓，会务全面停顿，会员星散。

4. 创办元甲中学

1948年《佛山精武会第二十届征求特刊》记录了佛山精武人

的感慨：“经过国民革命、抗日战争，精武会依然屹立不倒，此乃本会之幸、国家之幸，必须要有强健的体魄，才能战胜一切艰难困苦。”强健体魄之成者，首倡体育事业之加强。为实现精武会“专精惟一，乃武乃文”的宗旨，佛山精武会于精武国术学院原址创办元甲中学（又称“健社”），以德、智、体、美、群“五育”为办学宗旨。

（七）佛山精武体育会第二次复会

（梁旭辉整理）

佛山精武会在1986年第二次复会，与1921年创会、1946年抗日战争胜利后第一次复会共同成为佛山武术史上具有历史意义的时间节点。佛山精武会以中山公园永久会址为场地，积极开展传统武术整理、传承工作，举办了各种武术培训班和比赛，令以城区为龙头的佛山武术文化走上复兴之路。

operation of the Association stopped completely and its members were scattered.

4. The establishment of Yuanjia Middle School

The Twelfth Special Issue of Foshan Jingwu Association published in 1948 records the emotions of Foshan Jingwu people, "After the National Revolution and the War of Resistance against Japanese Aggression, the Jingwu Association still stands upright. This is a blessing for the Association and for the country. It is essential to have a strong physique to overcome all difficulties and setbacks." The first step to do so was to enhance sports endeavors. In order to fulfill its goal of "devotion, dedication, and integration of arts and arms", Foshan Jingwu Association established Yuanjia Middle School (also called Fitness Society) at the original site of Foshan Martial Arts Academy, advocating moral, intellectual, sports, aesthetic and social-skill education.

VII. The second resumption of Foshan Jingwu Association

(sorted by Liang Xuhui)

Foshan Jingwu Association was resumed for the second time in 1986. This resumption, its establishment in 1921 and its first resumption in 1946 after the victory of the War of Resistance against Japanese Aggression, have become historic moments in the history of Foshan martial arts. On its permanent site Sun Yat-sen Park, Foshan Jingwu Association has actively sorted out and inherited traditional martial arts and held various martial arts training classes and activities, so the martial arts culture in Foshan with the city proper as the hub has been rejuvenated.

3.2 Nan Jia Quan

I. History of Nan Jia Quan

Nan Jia Quan (the Nan Family Fist) was introduced into Guangdong in the mid to late Qing Dynasty and into Foshan in the late Qing Dynasty and the Republic of China. As it was created a long time ago, it is impossible to trace its origin. It was known to be popular among the martial monks in Southern Shaolin temple in the Ming and Qing dynasties.

In the mid to late Qing Dynasty, Zen Master Mide, the third-generation successor of Nan Jia Quan, lived in seclusion in Maitreya Temple in the Baiyun Mountain in Guangzhou and secretly taught the skills among the monks of the Temple.

Master Mide was the teacher of Liang Xisu, a great master of Nan Jia Quan in Foshan.

Liang Xisu had numerous students, who passed down his skills till today.

Liang Xisu was originally named Liang Zhanying. His ancestral home was in Huangtian Village, Shunde. He was born in Foshan in 1872. When he was seven, he went to learn martial arts and orthopedic medicine from Master Mide at the Maitreya Temple. After eight years, he learned all the skills and became the fourth-generation successor of Nan Jia Quan and the founding father of the Foshan Nan Jia Quan.

In the 13th year of the Guangxu period (1887) of the Qing Dynasty, the 15-year-old Liang Xisu left the Temple and went to work for the Wu family, one of the five wealthiest families in Guangzhou. At the recommendation of his host

第二节　南家拳

（一）南家拳历史源流

南家拳于清代中晚期传入广东，晚清和民国时期流传于佛山。南家拳因创始年代久远，无法考其根源。其在明清时期流传于南少林寺的武僧之中。

清中晚期，南家拳第三代传人秘德禅师隐居于广州白云山弥勒寺，秘密传授技艺于寺院僧侣之中。

秘德禅师是佛山南家拳一代宗师梁细苏的师傅。

梁细苏弟子众多，技艺流传至今。

梁细苏，原名梁湛英，祖籍顺德黄田村，1872年出生于佛山。7岁时梁细苏到广州白云山弥勒寺随师学习武功及跌打医术，历经8年，尽得其师衣钵真传，成为南家拳第四代传人、佛山南家拳开山师祖。

清光绪十三年（1887），15岁的梁细苏技成下山，在广州五大家族之伍氏处打工，在东家伍慕贤引荐下，拜护院总管毕六（花县“铁手”毕南春之徒）为师，兼习洪拳。曾为维护伍家人的生命财

南家拳
Nan Jia Quan

Wu Muxian, he learned Hong Quan from Bi Liu, the head guard of the family. Bi Liu used to learn from Bi Nanchun, the "Iron Hand" of Huaxian County. In order to protect the lives and property of the Wu family, Liang once fought against ten people by himself, so he made his name in Guangzhou and was called "Iron Fist Liang Xisu".

In the 20th year of the Guangxu period (1894) of the Qing Dynasty, the 22-year-old Liang was invited to the celebration ceremony at Taibao Temple in Xiguan, Guangzhou and performed martial arts together with Huang Feihong, Lin Shirong, Cheng Hua, Huang Manrong, Zhang Ju and Baitoubao.

On November 11th, 1947, *Nanhai Daily* carried a piece of news about the competition between Yip Man and Liang Xisu. It shows that in the 1940s, Liang was already a household name in Foshan for his peerless martial arts skills and martial arts learners thought it an honor to compete with him.

Liang Xisu "made his living with his orthopedic skills at Yingzuisha (now southeast of Sun Yat-sen Park in Foshan) in the early period of the Republic of China and established a gymnasium to teach apprentices. Later he moved it to the town and enrolled numerous students" [1].

His students who are still alive include Huang Weili (82 years old) and Chen Nianfeng (77 years old) in Foshan. The successors of his other students' are distributed in different districts of Foshan, and in Guangzhou and abroad.

II. Procedure and symbols of entry to Nan Jia Quan

Nan Jia Quan still retains the ancient charm of traditional martial arts, without any fancy tricks.

1. Ancestral precepts

The codes read, "First, teaching; second, practicing; third, flexibility; fourth, peace; fifth, modesty; sixth, harmony, seventh, favorable location; eighth, endurance; ninth, imitation of deities; tenth, perseverence; eleventh, adherence

1 Ou Ruizhi. *New Developments in Foshan*. Nanhai Serial Printing Company. 1992, p.197.

to foundation; and twelfth, equal focus on arms and arts.

2. Becoming a student

When one wants to become a student, he has to first offer pork, mutton, beef, and fruits as sacrifices to Emperor Guan and burn joss sticks. Then he has to present his apprentice letter to establish the teacher-student relationship.

3. Initial teaching of fist and stake skills

The dates for the masters to start the initial teaching of fist and stake skills must fall on some "Heavenly Pardon Days". The date for the latter is set in late spring or early summer, when the climate is getting warmer and the human sweat glands are more active. When the skin is rubbed against the wooden dummy, the sweat can serve as a lubricant to protect the skin and muscles, which conforms to the natural law of harmony between heaven and man.

4. The master's precepts

Nan Jia Quan is an internal martial arts type of Southern Shaolin Temple, featuring swiftness, flexibility and uniqueness. Liang Xisu treasured it especially so he attached great importance to the integrity of his students, which can be known from the precepts recorded by his students (omitted).

5. Special symbols of Nan Jia Quan—gestures, code words and the fist type symbol

As Nan Jia Quan was closely related to secret organizations to oppose the Qing and restore the Ming, its people had their unique ways of communicating with each other, which were similar to those of the Heaven and Earth Society. In the meantime, they also had their own features.

(1)Gestures

In the past, when the members of Nan Jia Quan were communicating with each other, one would make the gesture of "half a coin" with one hand. If the other was a fellow man, he would make the same gesture in return, so the two gestures could form the shape of a whole coin. This was a unique gesture used by Nan Jia Quan people.

(2)Code words

The question-and-answer form was adopted to explore whether the other was one's fellow man. If their code words matched, their identities were confirmed.

产以一敌十，名震羊城，人称“铁拳梁细苏”。

清光绪二十年（1894），22岁的梁细苏应邀参加西关太保庙贺诞，与黄飞鸿、林世荣、程华、黄满荣、张居、白头保等同台献技。

1947年11月11日《南海日报》载“叶问与梁细苏赛事”消息一则，从其内容可知，20世纪40年代，梁细苏已是佛山武术名师，其绝世武功在民间流传，学武者也以能与梁细苏切磋技艺为幸事。

中年时的梁细苏（李荣供图）
Middle-aged Liang Xisu (photo provided by Li Rong)

梁细苏于“民国初始在鹰嘴沙（今佛山中山公园外东南侧）以跌打医术为业，设馆授徒，后迁馆于镇内传技，门徒甚众”[1]。

如今梁细苏亲传弟子仍健在的，有佛山的黄伟立（82岁）和陈年丰（77岁）两人。其他弟子的传人分布于佛山各区、广州，以及海外。

1 区瑞芝：《佛山新语》，南海系列印刷公司1992年版，第197页。

（二）南家拳入门程式及标记

该拳种依然保留着传统武术的古朴韵味，没有花巧，极具民间气息。

1. 祖训

口诀：“一，师；二，练；三，灵变；四，海升平；五，要谦；六，合人和；七，讲地利；八，门忍气；九，效神仙；十，但得河水浅，明日到潭关，孔家无二派，临阵见艰难；十一，树高千丈，落叶归根；十二，世上有文须重武、文武双全天下徒。”

2. 拜师

门徒正式拜师时，首先要备三牲、供花果、烧香烛、奉关帝，而后求学者呈上拜师帖，确立师徒关系。

3. 开拳开桩

南家拳师傅向弟子初授拳法（“开拳”）和初授桩法（“开桩”），必须选择“天赦日”。开桩选春末夏初时节，这时气候转暖，人体汗腺分泌更旺，气血充盈，人体皮肤与木人桩进行摩擦，汗液起到润滑作用，保护了皮肤与肢体肌肉，顺应了天人合一的自然规律。

4. 师嘱

南家拳为南少林内家拳种，疾极灵变，拳法独特。梁细苏对南家拳珍重有加，在择徒方面尤为注重人品，从其门徒记录的师嘱（从略），可见一斑。

(3)The fist type symbol

The *Yin* and *Yang* Diagram has been an important and unique symbol of Nan Jia Quan. Liang Xisu passed it on as a token, representing his wish and expectations of the spread and flourishing of the fist type.

III. Major technical styles and characteristics of Nan Jia Quan

There are four things to bear in mind when practicing Nan Jia Quan: head rising up, finger tips pointing skyward, shoulders sinking, and *qi* sinking to Dantian(Dantian is a Taoist term, which is divided into upper, middle and lower Dantian. Here it refers to the lower Dantian. i.e. the lower abdomen). The hand movements must be skewed, crooked, and fast. Soft bridge hands must be responded with hard hitting and hard bridge hands defeated with tenderness. The hands and feet must act together and coordinately, striking forcefully and flexibly. Cleverness can beat clumsiness. Tenderness and hardness should work with each other, and internal and external forces should be combined for hard, rapid and coherent actions and bursts of power.

IV. Traditional routines of Nan Jia Quan

1. Freehand fighting

There are mainly Lohan Undressing and Tiger Subduing Fist, Guanping Holding the Seal Fist, Iron Bow Three-Wire Fist (also called Master Iron Three Rolling Fist), Flower Fist, Flower Hammer and Ten-Shape Fist.

20世纪40年代梁细苏弟子邓诵传抄的"铁公三辊正拳"拳谱

The manuscript of Master Iron Three Rolling Fist copied by Deng Song, a student of Liang Xisu's in the 1940s

2. Main weapon routines

There are mainly Two-Tiger Row-Teeth Benches, Two-Tiger Row-Teeth Swords, Two-Tiger Stakes, Five-Dragon Broadswords, Five-Tiger Dragon Swords, Wind-Wheel Swords, Single Swords, *Yin* and *Yang* Windmill Sticks, Defeating Luo Cheng Throat-Locking Spears, Blocking-Tiger-from-Returning-to-Forest Sticks, 108 Methods in Wooden Dummy Training (including 36 Heaven Methods and 72 Earth Methods), 41 Positive Stakes, Immortal Zhongli's Fans, hoes, Spring and Autumn Broadswords, Eight Immortals' Sabers, Single Fans, Six-Point-Five Clubs, Weituo Whips and Shoulder Poles.

V. Major representative successors of Nan Jia Quan

1. Qin Hai's branch

Qin Hai (1918-2000) was from Kezhuang Village, Nan'gang, Huangpu, Guangzhou. He was one of the early teaching assistants to Liang Xisu and had numerous students.

2. Li Jinning's branch

Li Jinning (1906-1966) was from Panyu, Guangzhou. He loved martial arts and lion dancing techniques since young. He was one of Liang Xisu's favorite disciples and capable assistants. He had numerous students.

3. Yuan En's branch

Yuan En (1916-2010) was a native of Dongguan, Guangdong, whose family lived in Foshan for generations. He adored martial arts and had profound understanding of martial arts philosophy. With a solid foundation, he had long served as a teaching assistant to Liang Xisu, imparting techniques to many younger fellow students on Liang's behalf.

4. Huang Anzhi's branch

Huang Anzhi (1911-1988), a native of Shangsha, Foshan, was born in a family of traditional Chinese medicine. In 1930, he became a student of Liang Xisu's to learn Nan Jia Quan and orthopedic medicine. He was skilled at over 30 fist and weapon routines and was especially good at analyzing martial arts theories.

5. 南家拳门派特殊标记——手语、暗语、拳种标记

南家拳与反清复明秘密组织相关，其门人联络方式与天地会这一庞大组织有类似之处，却又有其独特的地方。

（1）手语

昔日南家拳同门联络，以“半钱”为标记——单手摆出半个铜钱的形状，对方如是同门，必定意会，也会以单手摆出一个相对应的“半钱”形状，两者相合为一完整的铜钱形状，这是南家拳门人特有的联络手语。

（2）暗语

以一问一答形式，探知对方是否为同门中人，暗语对上，即为同门。

（3）拳种标记

两仪图一直作为该拳种的重要标志。梁细苏以此作为门派的独特标志，传作信物，代表了他对该拳种传播繁衍的心愿与期许。

（三）南家拳主要技术风格和特色

南家拳练拳四要：头昂灌顶，指尾撑天，吞肩落膊，气下丹田（丹田，道教用语，有上、中、下丹田，此应指下丹田，在脐下小腹处）。出手要斜、歪、快，柔桥刚打，刚桥柔制。手与脚同，脚与手齐，以力为基础，以活为主，以巧制拙，以快为主；软硬兼施，内外结合，刚猛快速，动作连贯，力量爆发。

（四）南家拳主要传统套路

1. 徒手拳术

主要有罗汉卸衣伏虎拳、关平抱印拳、铁弓三线拳（又名“铁公三辗拳”）、花拳、花捶、十形拳等。

2. 器械套路

主要有二虎排牙凳、二虎排牙刀、二虎桩、五龙大刀、五虎现龙刀、演风轮剑、单刀、两仪风车棍、罗成败北锁喉枪、截虎归林棍、木人桩法一百零八手（包含三十六天罡手法、七十二地煞手法）、四十一正桩、汉钟离扇、锄头、春秋大刀、八仙剑、单扇、六点半棍、韦陀鞭、担竿棍种等。

（五）南家拳主要代表传人

1. 秦海支线

秦海（1918—2000），广州黄埔南岗柯庄村人，是梁细苏早年的助教之一，弟子众多。

2. 李锦宁支线

李锦宁（1906—1966），广州番禺人，自幼喜爱武术和醒狮技艺，为梁细苏的得意门徒和得力助手，弟子甚众。

3. 袁恩支线

袁恩（1916—2010），祖籍广东东莞，世居佛山，崇尚武术。他对拳理与南家拳内法有较深刻的理解，根基扎实，长期担任梁细

南家拳
Nan Jia Quan

5. Huang Nianfa's branch

Huang Nianfa (1927-1978), was from Shangbai, Luocun, Foshan. In the early 1940s, he learned martial arts at the martial arts gymnasium run by Chen Tian, a student of Liang Xisu's. In 1946, he learned from Liang Xisu. His son and numerous students pass on his techniques.

6. Li Lai's branch

Li Lai (1919-1989) was from Hexi Village, Xiqiao, the former Nanhai County and lived in Foshan. In 1937, he became a student of Liang Xisu's and was most proficient in the footwork of Nan Jia Quan. Li Lai's branch spreads the martial art to Xiqiao of Nanhai and Xi'nan of Sanshui. Li's students include Li Qiang (his son), Wu Huiping, Liang Wandeng, and others.

7. Deng Song's branch

Deng Song (1914-1976), a native of the former Sanshui County and lived in Foshan. In 1941, he became a student of Liang Xisu's and acquired the internal skills of Nan Jia Quan and orthopedic medicine. He passed on Eight Immortals' Swords and Six-Point-Five Clubs to his son Deng Guoliang.

8. Chen Tian's branch

Chen Tian (years of birth and death unknown), was one of Liang Xisu's early students. He once established a martial arts gymnasium in Jiujiangji, Shangsha, Foshan. In 1943, he imparted Nan Jia Quan to Peng Nan, a notable Foshan Yongchun Quan master. In the 1980s, Peng Nan sorted out martial arts manuals and shot photos to demonstrate the skills for future generations.

9. Liu Xin's branch

Liu Xin (1913-1994) learned Nan Jia Quan from Liang Xisu in the 1930s. He was once a member of Guangzhou Martial Arts Team. He was among Liang's students who first established a gymnasium to teach Nan Jia Quan. He had coached a large number of students.

10. Huang Weili's branch

Huang Weili, was born in the former Shunde County in 1936 and settled in Foshan since his adolescence. In 1950, he became a student of Liang Xisu's. Even in his declining years, he is still concerned about the inheritance of Nan Jia Quan and supportive of the younger generations. He has kept practicing Nan Jia

苏的助教，并代师传艺，指导过许多师弟。

4. 黄安芝支线

黄安芝（1911—1988），世居佛山上沙，出身于中医世家。1930年，拜梁细苏为师，学习南家拳及跌打医术。熟习各种拳术器械30余套，尤重拳理剖析。

5. 黄年发支线

黄年发（1927—1978），广东佛山罗村上柏人。20世纪40年代初，他在梁细苏的弟子陈添的武馆学艺，1946年师从梁细苏，其子及众弟子传其艺。

6. 李来支线

李来（1919—1989），原南海县西樵河溪村人，定居佛山。1937年拜入梁细苏门下，南家拳脚法最精。李来支线将南家拳传播至南海西樵和三水西南，弟子有李强（李来之子）、吴惠平、梁万邓等。

7. 邓诵支线

邓诵（1914—1976），广东原三水县人，定居佛山。1941年，拜入梁细苏门下，学得南家拳内家功法和跌打医术，传子邓国梁八仙剑、六点半棍法。

8. 陈添支线

陈添，生卒年不详，是梁细苏早年的弟子，曾在佛山上沙九江基开设武馆。佛山咏春拳名师彭南曾在1943年师从陈添学南家拳。20世纪80年代，彭南整理拳谱，拍摄示范拳照，留存后世。

9. 刘新支线

刘新（1913—1994），20世纪30年代师从梁细苏学习南家拳，曾参加广州武术队。他是梁细苏弟子中较早设馆传授南家拳者之一，授徒多人。

10. 黄伟立支线

黄伟立，1936年出生于原顺德县，少年时定居佛山。1950年拜入梁细苏门下学艺。年迈仍心系南家拳的传承，扶掖后进，每天坚持习练南家拳，数十年从未间断。弟子有秦伟彪、李泽光、梁伟焯、黄志明等。

（六）南家拳传承现状与保护价值

进入21世纪，随着佛山对自身武术历史的调查挖掘，南家拳多年分散的力量得以聚集。2004年起，为加强海内外南家拳传人的沟通，南家拳传人每年召开联谊大会，以武术为纽带，凝聚海内外力量，宣传和传播中华传统武术文化。2010年，佛山市武术协会南家拳会成立。

1. 历史价值

佛山南家拳涵盖传统南派武术和跌打医术，内涵丰富，资源丰厚。佛山南家拳由宗师梁细苏传入佛山，流传至今已有百年历史，它与洪拳、咏春拳、蔡李佛拳一样，为佛山南派武术中体系完备并富有独特风采的拳种。

Quan every day for several decades on end. His students include Qin Weibiao, Li Zeguang, Liang Weizhuo, Huang Zhiming and others.

VI. The status quo and importance of protecting Nan Jia Quan

In the 21st century, with efforts to explore the history of Foshan martial arts, forces of Nan Jia Quan which have been scattered for many years have been congregated. Since 2004, in order to enhance communication among successors of Nan Jia Quan in Foshan and other parts of the world, an annual meeting of friendship is held to pool domestic and international forces together, and publicize and disseminate traditional martial arts culture with martial arts as a link. In 2010, Nan Jia Quan Society under Foshan Martial Arts Association was established.

梁伟焯在南家拳馆传授南家拳棍法（梁伟焯供图）
Liang Weizhuo teaching Nan Jia Quan Clubs at Nan Jia Quan Gymnasium (photo provided by Liang himself)

1. Historical value

Nan Jia Quan in Foshan covers both traditional southern martial arts and orthopedic medicine, with rich connotations and abundant resources. Since Liang Xisu first introduced it into Foshan, it has been spreading in the city for over a century. Like Hong Quan, Yongchun Quan and Cai Li Fo Quan, it is a type of southern martial arts in Foshan with a complete system and its own charm .

2. Scientific value

Nan Jia Quan of Foshan uses "shape and shadow" to explain its martial arts theories. Master Liang Xisu's oral precepts of martial arts maintain, "It is difficult to withdraw the shadow when there is shape but no shadows: it is difficult to capture the shape when there is shadow but no shape". This shows the related actions in martial arts movements and the application of shape and shadow. It is important to determine the force of life and death when striking, which involves the scientific law of unity of opposites such as pompous versus practical, hard versus soft, intense versus relaxing, and fast versus slow.

3. Cultural values

Nan Jia Quan of Foshan stresses clearness, quietness, and steadiness. Clearness facilitates understanding; quietness generates intelligence and steadiness makes one at ease.

2. 科学价值

佛山南家拳以“形影”诠释拳理。宗师梁细苏的口传拳论指出“有形无影难收影，有影无形难擒形”，这是对于武术运动变化过程中关联动作的一种表述，说明对于形影不离关系的运用，要求出手定分生死力，这就包含了浮与实、刚与柔、张与弛、快与慢的科学道理。

3. 文化价值

佛山南家拳师传“清、静、定”，“清”可明理，“静”能生智，“定”则从容。

第三节　太极拳

（一）太极拳历史渊源

太极拳是极富中华民族传统特色元素的文化形态。太极始于无极，分两仪，由两仪分三才，由三才显四象，既而演变八卦。依据《易经》阴阳之理、中医经络学、道家导引术、吐纳法综合创造的一套有阴阳性质、符合人体结构和大自然运转规律的拳术，古人称之为“太极”。

17世纪中叶，河南温县陈家沟陈王廷（1600—1680）在家传拳法的基础上，吸收众家武术之长，融合易学、中医等思想，创编出一套具有阴阳开合、刚柔相济、内外兼修特色的拳法，命名为太极拳。太极拳在陈家沟世代传承。

自后人陈长兴（1771—1853）起，太极拳开始向外传播，后逐渐衍生出以杨露禅（1799—1872）为代表的杨式太极拳、以吴鉴泉（1870—1942）为代表的吴式太极拳、以孙禄堂（1860—1933）为代表的孙式太极拳和以武禹襄（1812—1880）为代表的武式太极拳等多家流派。太极拳成为当今中国武坛上传承最广的拳种。

3.3 Taiji Quan

I. History of Taiji Quan

Taiji Quan is a cultural form rich in characteristic traditional Chinese elements. *Taiji* (t'ai chi) starts from infinity and is divided into *yin* and *yang*, which are separated into three talents, from which four phenomena are displayed and changed into *Bagua* (eight diagrams). Based on the theory of *yin* and *yang* of *Yi Jing* (*The Book of Changes*), the channel theory of traditional Chinese medicine, and the guidance and respiration methods of Taoism, *Taiji* was created, featuring the quality of both *yin* and *yang* and conformity to the body structure and the law of nature.

In the mid-17th century, Chen Wangting (1600-1680) from Chenjiagou, Wenxian County, Henan Province created a new set of martial arts called Taiji Quan. Based on his family martial arts, Taiji Quan had taken advantage of other martial arts skills and integrated the theories of *Yi Jing* and traditional Chinese medicine, thus featuring the opening and closing of *yin* and *yang*, the combination of hardness and softness, and the improvement of both internal and external quality. Taiji Quan was passed down from generation to generation in Chenjiagou.

Chen Changxing (1771-1853) started spreading Taiji Quan from Chenjiagou to other places. Later many schools were derived from it, such as those represented by Yang Luchan (1799-1872), Wu Jianquan (1870-1942), Sun Lutang (1860-1933), and Wu Yuxiang (1812-1880). It has become the most widely spread martial arts type in China.

太极拳
Taiji Quan

（二）最早传入佛山的吴式太极拳

最早传入佛山的太极拳，是由吴鉴泉、徐致一在上海精武体育会传播的吴式太极拳。

经常到上海开会的精武委员会主要成员李佩弦、任孝安、林君选，以及教练蔡丽秋、招天爵等人，就是佛山最早学习吴式太极拳的学员，他们是将太极拳这个拳种传入佛山的第一批本地教练。

（三）20世纪40年代传入的杨式太极拳

佛山精武体育会会员区荣钜是佛山第一个接触杨式太极拳的学生，他与杨式太极拳的传入有直接的联系。

1930年，区荣钜正式加入佛山精武体育会，学习北方长拳、鹰爪拳、螳螂拳、精武十套拳等，最早是李佩弦、蔡丽秋、何心平等在会中传授吴式太极拳，他从学其中，对太极有了一定的了解。后拜师石再贤、杨守中，受教于香港董英杰，学习杨式太极拳。

1953年起，区荣钜开始传授太极拳，学生有万余人，徒子徒孙遍及海内外。

2012年，区荣钜去世。

（四）20世纪50年代传入的张金龄太极拳

20世纪50年代，张金龄太极拳传入佛山。它既有杨式太极拳姿势舒展、身法中正的特点，也有吴式太极拳松静自然、重柔善化的特点，还有李式太极拳体松缓慢、连贯灵活的特点。在拳术运用上以静伺动，先化后打；趁势借力，即化即打；腾挪闪战，不化亦打。张金龄太极拳讲究稳、圆、匀、柔，其拳法要求“用意不用力，运动绕螺旋，内外重六合，源泉在丹田”，既有各式太极拳的共性，又独具特色。

1. 张金龄太极拳的始创

张金龄太极拳创始人是清末民初的云南太极一代宗师张金龄，人称“张太极”。

张金龄（1877—1960），字寿轩，河北宁津县张家寨人。自幼从父亲张宏生（李瑞东弟子）学习太极拳，后拜在吴式太极拳创始人吴鉴泉和李式太极拳创始人李瑞东（1851—1917）门下苦练，并系统继承了李瑞东医术。张金龄将平生所学融会贯通，熔冶一炉，逐渐形成独具个人风格和特色的太极拳，年轻时便成名于京师。因为战乱，张金龄于1930年携大弟子周瑞木经湖南长沙、贵州贵阳至云南昆明行医授拳并定居，在昆明维新街开设骨科中医诊所。张金龄是将太极拳传入云南的第一人，是云南太极拳发展史上一个里程碑式的人物。张金龄在全国有众多弟子，如台湾陶炳祥（五柳堂创始人）和高子安、广东佛山黎日晴、四川宋金辉、湖南黄尧熙、河北高瑞奇等。

II. The Wu-style Taiji Quan, the first introduced into Foshan

The first that was introduced into Foshan is the Wu-style Taiji Quan disseminated by Wu Jianquan and Xu Zhiyi at Shanghai Jingwu Sports Association.

Major Jingwu Committee members such as Li Peixian, Ren Xiao'an and Lin Junxuan and coaches such as Cai Liqiu and Zhao Tianjue, who often attended meetings in Shanghai were the first to learn the Wu-style Taiji Quan and also the first batch of coaches to introduce it into Foshan.

III. The Yang-style Taiji Quan, introduced into Foshan in the 1940s

Ou Rongju, a member of Foshan Jingwu Sports Association, was the first student in Foshan to learn the Yang-style Taiji Quan and was directly related to its introduction into Foshan.

In 1930, Ou formally joined Foshan Jingwu Sports Association and practiced Northern Long Fist, Eagle Claw Fist, Mantis Fist, and Jingwu Ten-Set Fist. At the beginning, Ou learned the Wu-style Taiji Quan taught by Li Peixian, Cai Liqiu and He Xinping in the Association. Later he learned the Yang-style Taiji Quan from Shi Zaixian and Yang Shouzhong as well as Dong Yingjie from Hong Kong.

Since 1953, Ou Rongju started teaching Taiji Quan, his students totaling over 10,000 and spreading all over the world.

Ou passed away in 2012.

IV. Zhang Jinling Taiji Quan, introduced into Foshan in the 1950s

In the 1950s, Zhang Jinling Taiji Quan was introduced into Foshan. It has the features of a stretched posture and an upright body of the Yang style; of the looseness, naturalness, softness and adaptability of the Wu style; and of the looseness, slowness, coherence and flexibility of the Li style. In the use of fist techniques, it emphasizes remaining still before taking actions and disintegrating offence before striking; taking advantage of the situation to disintegrate offence and to strike; dodging attacks with quick counterattacks to strike without disintegrating offence. Featuring steadiness, roundness, evenness and softness, its skills require "the use of mind instead of force, spiral movement, an emphasis on *Liuhe* (six harmonies) both internally and externally, and sources at *Dantian*". Zhang Jinling Taiji Quan has not only the commonalities of different styles, but also its unique characteristics.

1. Creation of Zhang Jinling Taiji Quan

The creator Zhang Jinling was a great master of Yunnan Taiji Quan in the late Qing Dynasty and the early Republic of China, nicknamed "Zhang Taiji".

Zhang Jinling (1877-1960), also called Zhang Shouxuan, was from Zhangjiazhai, Ningjin County, Hebei Province. Since young, he learned Taiji Quan from his father Zhang Hongsheng, a student of Li Ruidong's. Later he learned from Wu Jianquan, the creator of the Wu-style Taiji Quan, and also from Li Ruidong (1851-1917), the creator of the Li-style Taiji Quan and systematically inherited Li's medical skills. Zhang Jinling integrated all he had learned and gradually formed his own style of Taiji Quan. He made his name in the capital Beijing when he was young. In 1930, because of war, Zhang, together with his first student Zhou Ruimu, passed Changsha in Hunan and Guiyang in Guizhou to practice medicine and teach martial arts in Kunming, Yunnan. He operated an orthopedic traditional Chinese medicine clinic on Weixin Street, Kunming. Zhang was the first person to introduce Taiji Quan into Yunnan and a milestone figure in the history of Taiji Quan in Yunnan. He had numerous students around the country, such as Tao Bingxiang (the founder of Taiwan Wuliu Hall) and Gao Zi'an from Taiwan, Li Riqing from Foshan of Guangdong, Song Jinhui from Sichuan, Huang Yaoxi from Hunan, and Gao Ruiqi from Hubei.

2. Dissemination of Zhang Jinling Taiji Quan in Foshan

It was Li Riqing who introduced Zhang Jinling Taiji Quan into Foshan.

Li Riqing (1908-2003) was a native of the former Nanhai County, whose family lived in Foshan for generations. He loved martial arts since young.

In 1927, he joined Foshan Jingwu Sports Association. During the War of Resistance against Japanese Aggression, he and his family moved to Kunming,

太极拳

Taiji Quan

2. 张金龄太极拳在佛山的传承

将张金龄太极拳传入佛山的是黎日晴。

黎日晴（1908—2003），广东原南海县人，世居佛山，自幼喜爱武术。

1927年，黎日晴加入佛山精武体育会习武。抗日战争期间，为避战乱举家迁往云南昆明。1944年，黎日晴在昆明偶遇张金龄，得知张金龄乃云南太极名家，慕其太极拳艺，拜于张金龄门下系统学习太极拳。1958年，黎日晴回佛山定居，在佛山传播张金龄太极拳。

20世纪50—70年代，黎日晴曾在佛山新广场开设多个张金龄太极拳学习班。1986年，黎日晴参与佛山精武体育会复会工作，除了传授精武十套基本拳之外，还把张金龄太极拳传授给会员，受众达千人次之多。

（五）20世纪60年代后推广的简化太极拳

20世纪60年代，中华人民共和国体育运动委员会在全国范围内推广简化太极拳健身运动，这是为强健人民群众身体而创编的简单易学的太极拳套路，对改善国民体质起到了较好作用。在其后的几十年中，简化太极拳推广和流行之迅速、学练人数之多，也是其他拳种无法比拟的。

Yunnan. In 1944, Li met Zhang Jinling in Kunming and came to know that Zhang was a great Taiji Quan master in Yunnan. Admiring Zhang's Taiji Quan skills, Li became his student for systematic learning. In 1958, Li went back to settle in Foshan and started disseminating Zhang Jinling Taiji Quan.

In the 1950s to 1970s, Li Riqing used to offer Taiji Quan training classes at New Square of Foshan. In 1986, Li helped with the work to resume Foshan Jingwu Sports Association. Apart from the basic Jingwu Ten-Set Fist, he also taught Zhang Jinling Taiji Quan to its members, who amounted to over 1,000 people.

V. Simplified Taiji Quan, promoted since the 1960s

In the 1960s the State Sports Commission publicized simplified Taiji Quan nationwide, which aimed at and succeeded in strengthening the health of the people. In the subsequent decades, the simplified Taiji Quan has witnessed matchless speed of dissemination and numbers of learners when compared with other martial arts types.

VI. The Chen-style Taiji Quan, introduced into Foshan in the 1980s

The Chen-style Taiji Quan, the source of all types of Taiji Quan, originated from Chenjiagou, Wenxian County, Henan Province. It was passed down from generation to generation. It was introduced into Foshan in the 1980s and was popularized in the 1990s.

In 1995, Chen Youhua, whose elder brother was Chen Youqin (the 18th generation offspring at Chenjiagou and the 12th generation successor of the Chen-style Taiji Quan, came to Foshan Jingwu Sports Association. With the help of its vice presidents Huang Yingxin and Zheng Ling and the President of Foshan Taiji Quan Research Association Zeng Kun, the first training class of the Chen-style Taiji Quan, enrolled by Foshan Jingwu Association, was carried out in Foshan Amusement Park. The Chen-style Taiji Quan was then gradually popularized.

VII. National promotion of Taiji Quan competitions

In the 1980s, Taiji Quan, Taiji sword and Taiji pushing hands were the only national competitions that were named according to martial arts types.
In 1986, the State Sports Commission separately listed Taiji Quan, Taiji sword and Taiji pushing hands as formal national competition items to be held annually. The competitions fall into three categories. First, Taiji Quan, divided into 42 styles, such as the Yang style, the Wu style, the Chen style and the Sun style. Second, competitive routines of Taiji sword. Third, Taiji pushing hands.

1993年，佛山市太极拳研究会会员在佛山乐园表演24式简化太极拳（曾秀珠供图）
Performance of 24-form simplified Taiji Quan by Foshan Taiji Quan Research Association members at Foshan Amusement Park in 1993 (photo provided by Zeng Xiuzhu)

VIII. Establishment of Foshan Taiji Quan Association

1. Establishment and organizational structure of Foshan Taiji Quan Association

Foshan Taiji Quan Association, formerly Foshan Taiji Quan Research Association, was founded on November 28, 1993. It is a registered non-profit social organization with legal person status in Foshan, formed voluntarily by Taiji Quan lovers. Its main business scopes include various Taiji Quan training

（六）20世纪80年代传入的陈式太极拳

陈式太极拳是各式太极拳运动之拳宗，发端于河南温县陈家沟，世代相传。

陈式太极拳于20世纪80年代中期传入佛山，20世纪90年代才开始普及。

1995年，陈家沟第十八世嫡孙、陈式太极拳第十二代传人陈有芹的弟弟陈友华来到佛山精武体育会，在佛山精武体育会副会长黄颖心、郑玲和佛山市太极拳研究会会长曾坤的帮助下，由佛山精武体育会招生，以佛山乐园为训练场，举办首届陈式太极拳培训班，自此陈式太极拳在群众中渐渐普及。

（七）太极拳竞赛全国推广

20世纪80年代，太极拳、剑、推手比赛是唯一按拳种命名的全国性比赛。

1986年，国家体育运动委员会将太极拳、剑、推手单列为全国正式比赛项目，每年举行一次。竞赛项目分为三类：一是太极拳，分为42式，即杨式太极拳、吴式太极拳、陈式太极拳、孙式太极拳等；二是太极剑竞赛套路；三是太极推手。

（八）佛山市太极拳协会创立

1. 佛山市太极拳协会创立及其组织架构

佛山市太极拳协会的前身是佛山市太极拳研究会，于1993年11月28日成立，是佛山市登记在册的社会团体法人，是由太极拳爱好者自愿组成的非营利性质的社会组织，主要业务范围是针对会员开展各种太极拳培训班、普及推广太极拳、开展太极拳研究和交流活动。

佛山市太极拳协会由理事会组织执行会务，下设表演队和各片区、辅导站。理事会成员和片长、站长由热心会员担任，全是义务承担责任。现届理事会设有6个部门（办公室、组织部、拓展部、竞训部、信息宣传部、保健部）。

2. 佛山市太极拳协会所传拳术种类及引进佛山的渠道

佛山市太极拳协会推广的拳种有传统的太极拳套路，也有原国家体育运动委员会、国家体育总局推广的基础和竞赛套路。传统的套路主要于20世纪20年代初随着佛山精武体育会传入，加上佛山市太极拳协会首任会长曾坤的不断创编，协会现在教学及表演的各种体育健身运动套路已有49套。近五年来，协会又将健身气功成功推广为佛山全民健身运动的新宠。

3. 佛山市太极拳协会传授拳术方式

协会秉承精武体育会“摒弃门户之见”的精神，对优秀传统武术项目兼容并包，倡导教学相长，注重根据学员的群体性和个性施教培养。协会设有教练考评制度，会员骨干学习规定套路并通过考

classes for its members, popularization and promotion of Taiji Quan, and research and exchange activities of Taiji Quan.

Foshan Taiji Quan Association is operated by its council, under which there are performance teams, various districts and counseling stations. Members of the council, heads of the districts and directors of the counseling stations are undertaken by enthusiastic members, who shoulder the responsibilities without any pay. The current council has six departments (the office, the organizing department, the expansion department, the competition and training department, the information and publicity department, and the healthcare department).

2. Types of Taiji Quan taught by Foshan Taiji Quan Association and their introduction channels

The types of Taiji Quan promoted by Foshan Taiji Quan Association include traditional Taiji Quan routines and basic and competitive routines promoted by the former State Sports Commission and the General Administration of Sport of China. The traditional ones mainly include those introduced into Foshan in the 1920s by Foshan Jingwu Sports Association. Together with those created by Zeng Kun, the first President of Foshan Taiji Quan Association, there are now 49 sets of sports and fitness routines taught and performed by the Association. In the recent five years, the Association has made *Qigong* (a system of breathing exercises) a new favorite sport for fitness among people in Foshan.

3. Modes of teaching in Foshan Taiji Quan Association

Adhering to the spirit of Jingwu Sports Association of "discarding the prejudice concerning different schools", Foshan Taiji Quan Association embraces various traditional martial arts items and advocates reciprocal development of teaching and learning by offering both group and individual training tailored to different learners. The Association is equipped with the coach assessment system, by means of which key members can be employed by the Association as coaches after learning the designated routines and passing the assessment.

4. Zeng Kun, the founding president of Foshan Taiji Quan Association

Zeng Kun was born in Foshan, Guangdong Province in 1928. In 1947 he joined Foshan Jingwu Sports Association and learned Eagle Claw Fist from

Liu Fameng, a great master from Hebei Province. In 1949, he was employed as a teaching assistant in Foshan Jingwu Sports Association. He used to be a member of the Foshan Committee of the CPPCC (the Chinese People's Political Consultative Conference), a council member of Guangdong Martial Arts Association, vice president of Foshan Jingwu Sports Association, vice president of Foshan Martial Arts Association, president of Taiji Quan Society of Foshan Martial Arts Association, and president of Eagle Claw Fist Society of Foshan Martial Arts Association. He is a national level-one referee and holds a certificate of the 6th rank in China's Martial Arts System.

Zeng Kun has trained more than 100 coaches and countless students. Because of his great efforts to popularize and develop Foshan traditional martial arts culture, his meritorious deeds have been carried in a number of monographs such as *Foshan Martial Arts Culture*, *A Dictionary of Martial Arts Masters in China*, and *Encyclopedia of Taiji Quan in China*. In recent years, Zeng Kun has been invited to demonstrate Taiji Quan and Eagle Claw Fist in a number of documentary movies such as *Longevity Code* and *The Tale of Chinese Medicine* by CCTV.

核后，由协会聘为教练。

4. 佛山市太极拳协会创会会长曾坤

曾坤，1928年出生于广东省佛山市。1947年加入佛山精武体育会，师从河北著名鹰爪拳大师刘法孟，学习鹰爪拳。1949年受聘为佛山精武体育会助教。曾任佛山市政协委员，广东省武术协会委员，佛山精武体育会副会长，佛山市武术协会副会长、武术协会太极拳会会长、武术协会鹰爪拳会会长等，国家一级裁判员，国家武术段位六段。

曾坤培养教练逾百名，学生弟子不计其数，大力推动佛山传统武术文化的普及与发展，其事迹被载入《佛山武术文化》《中国武术人名辞典》《中国太极拳大百科》等多本专著。近年曾坤更受邀参与录制多部大型纪录片，如中央电视台的《长寿密码》《本草中国》等，展示其太极拳、鹰爪拳等功夫。

第四节　鹰爪拳

（一）鹰爪拳历史源流

鹰爪拳，又称鹰爪翻子拳、鹰手拳、鹰爪派、鹰爪派翻子门、少林鹰爪翻子门等，相传是由南宋抗金名将岳飞所创。鹰爪拳是由岳氏散手和翻子拳有机融合发展而成的以“鹰爪”手形为显著特点的传统北派拳种。鹰爪拳属北派少林拳系，自宋至元、明，虽代有传人，却名言不彰，无从稽考。

近代鹰爪拳可考历史可追溯至晚清同治、光绪年间河北保定雄县人刘仕俊。刘仕俊晚年回乡，在孤庄头村将技艺传给族孙刘成有。刘成有把鹰爪拳传给三儿子刘启文和外甥陈子正。

民国8年（1919），陈子正技成后应卢炜昌、陈公哲等人之邀赴上海精武会任教，创设鹰爪派。后来，陈子正又派其侄陈国庆去武汉任教，其弟子由述孔、孙成之、郭成尧、杨炳文、刘法孟、鲍希勇、陈国俊等分别在东北、北京、广东、湖南、湖北、河南、上海等地，包括在黄埔军校内传授鹰爪拳，鹰爪拳遂在全国流行。1921年，陈子正受聘往香港任教3年，其间又受聘在新加坡传授鹰

3.4 Eagle Claw Fist

I. History of Eagle Claw Fist

Eagle Claw Fist is said to have been created by Yue Fei, a famous anti-Jin general in the Southern Song Dynasty. It is a traditional northern martial arts type which has integrated the Yue-style *Sanshou* (freehand fighting) and Overturning Fist, with the distinctive feature of "eagle claw" hand shapes. It belongs to Northern Shaolin Martial Arts. Though it was passed down from the Southern Song to the Yuan and Ming dynasties, no record could be found about the details.

Modern Eagle Claw Fist can be traced back to Liu Shijun from Xiongxian County, Baoding City, Hebei Province during the Tongzhi and Guangxu periods of the late Qing Dynasty. In his old age, Liu Shijun returned to his hometown Guzhuangtou Village and passed on the skills to his brother's grandson Liu Chengyou, who later passed them on to his third son Liu Qiwen and nephew Chen Zizheng.

In 1919, Chen Zizheng, after mastering the skills, went to teach Eagle Claw Fist at Shanghai Central Jingwu Sports Association at the invitation of Lu Weichang and Chen Gongzhe and created the school of Eagle Claw Fist. Later, Chen Zizheng sent his nephew Chen Guoqing to teach in Wuhan. His students You Shukong, Sun Chengzhi, Guo Chengyao, Yang Bingwen, Liu Fameng, Bao Xiyong, and Chen Guoju respectively taught Eagle Claw Fist in the Northeast of China, Beijing, Guangdong, Hunan, Hubei, Henan, and Shanghai, including Huangpu Military Academy. In 1921, Chen Zizheng was invited to teach in Hong Kong for three years, during which he was also invited to teach in Singapore. Chen's students Liu Zhanwu, Liang Zipeng, Liu Zhixiang, and Zhang Junting also taught it in Hong Kong and Southeast Asia, making it well-known overseas.

II. Eagle Claw Fist introduced into Foshan

In the early 1920s, it was introduced into Foshan via Shanghai Jingwu Sports Association. It is one of the northern martial arts types first introduced into Foshan and has thrived for nearly a hundred years in the city. During the Republic of China, a number of Foshan people, including Li Peixian and Huang Baixiang, learned Eagle Claw Fist at Shanghai Jingwu Sports Association, after which they taught it in Foshan. In 1921, Foshan Jingwu Sports Association was founded. In July 1923, Li Peixian was sent by Shanghai Jingwu Sports Association to be the head of the National Gymnastics Division of Foshan Jingwu Sports Association and to teach Eagle Claw Fist. On December 14, 1923, Li Baoying, the first Eagle Claw master outside Guangdong Province, came to teach the Fist in the Court Historian Mansion at Lianhuadi, Foshan, with Cai Liqiu as his teaching assistant. It attracted a large number of learners after one year's development.

In 1956, Huang Baixiang settled down in his hometown Shatou, Nanhai. In the following year, Huang started teaching Eagle Claw Fist, Mantis Fist, and Six-Harmony and Eight-Method Fist. In 1967, when Shatou Martial Arts Team was founded, Huang served as the coach. Now Eagle Claw Fist at Xiqiao, Nanhai has mainly been disseminated by Huang.

III. Inheritance and development

In the 1985 national campaign to excavate and sort out martial arts resources, Zeng Kun made preliminary excavation of Foshan Eagle Claw Fist and compiled *Records of Eagle Claw Fist Weapons*. Because of his outstanding achievements, Zeng was awarded as an "Advanced Individual" by the former State Sports

爪拳，其弟子刘占武、梁子鹏、刘致祥、张俊庭在香港和东南亚地区传授鹰爪拳，使鹰爪拳闻名于境外。

（二）鹰爪拳传入佛山

近代鹰爪拳于20世纪20年代初经上海精武会传入佛山，在佛山传承近百年，是较早传入佛山的北方拳种之一。民国时期，李佩弦、黄佰祥等多名佛山人先后在上海精武会学习鹰爪拳，艺成后返回佛山传艺。1921年佛山精武体育会成立，1923年7月李佩弦受上海精武会委派回佛山任国操部主任，在会内教授鹰爪拳。同年12月14日，第一个来到佛山的外省籍鹰爪拳拳师李宝英，在莲花地太史第内教授鹰爪拳，蔡丽秋任助教。经过一年的发展，学习鹰爪拳的会员越来越多。

1956年，黄佰祥回到家乡南海沙头。翌年，黄佰祥开始收徒传艺，教授鹰爪拳、螳螂拳、六合八法拳等拳术。1967年，沙头武术队成立，由黄佰祥任教练。现在南海西樵一带鹰爪拳主要为黄佰祥所传播。

（三）薪火相传

在1985年的全国武术挖掘整理运动中，曾坤对佛山鹰爪拳进行了初步的挖掘，整理出《鹰爪派拳械录》，并因突出表现获得国家体育运动委员会颁发的“先进个人”荣誉称号。为保护和弘扬鹰爪

鹰爪拳
Eagle Claw Fist

Commission. In 2011, in order to protect and develop its cultural treasure, Eagle Claw Fist Inheritance and Development Center under Foshan Jingwu Sports Association was founded. In 2012, Zeng Kun, his student Chen Jianzhi, and his daughter Zeng Xiuzhu initiated the establishment of Eagle Claw Fist Society under Foshan Martial Arts Association. In September 2015, Foshan Eagle Claw Fist was included in the List of the Fifth Batch of Foshan Intangible Cultural Heritage. In 2016, Eagle Claw Fist Association of Nanhai District, Foshan City and Eagle Claw Fist Association of Zumiao Street, Chancheng District were founded.

曾坤演示鹰爪拳（陈健志供图）
Zeng Kun demonstrating Eagle Claw Fist (photo provided by Chen Jianzhi)

Foshan is a major place to spread Eagle Claw Fist. It has spread from Foshan to Guangzhou and countries such as Singapore, Malaysia, Brunei, France, Canada, and Australia. Therefore, Foshan has become an important transit point of its southward and outward dissemination.

IV. Major routines of Eagle Claw Fist

Freehand fighting routines of Eagle Claw Fist practiced in Foshan mainly include Eagle Claws, Fifty-Way Continuous Fists, Ten-Way Walking Fists, Eight-Step Fists, Shaolin Beats, Taizu Fists, Eight-Step Beats, Front Eight-Face Beats, Rear Eight-Face Beats, Big Soft Palms, Small Soft Palms, Big Hero Fists, Small Hero Fists, Lohan Fists, Wild Goose Walking Fists, Four-Six Fists, Six-Harmony Fists, Plum Blossom Fists, Five-Tiger Fists, Five Leopards, Front Slips, Drunken Liu Tang, 108 Hands, and Paired Soft Palms. Weapon routines include Big Chain Swords, Small Chain Swords, Plum Blossom Knives, Six-Harmony Knives, Chain Knives, Snowflake Double Swords, Plum Blossom Double Swords, Ground-Lying Double Swords, *Qimen*(unorthordox) Clubs, Eyebrow-

High Clubs, Chain Spears, Lohan Spears, Plum Blossom Spears, Six-Harmony Spears, Spring and Autumn Broadswords, Four-Gate Broadswords, Single Broadswords versus Spears, Double Broadswords versus Spears, and Sparring of Tiger-Catching Spears.

V. Celebrities and great masters of Eagle Claw Fist

1. Liu Shijun

Liu Shijun (1840-1910) was from Guzhuangtou Village, Xiongxian County, Hebei Province. He loved martial arts since young. Later he became a student of Master Facheng's to learn the Yue-style Continuous Fist (later called Eagle Claw Continuous Fist), Three-Step Spears, Five-Step Spears, Winding Spears, Strung Spears, Sparrow Hawk Spears, and Five-Way Big Spears. He also learned Eagle Claw Arresting Skills from Monk Daoji (Facheng's senior fellow student). Three years later, Liu left his teachers to travel around. He spent his whole life studying and teaching martial arts, which made him a well-known name in the country. Because he excelled in using big poles, he was called "Big Pole Liu". Later he served as a coach of the Escort Army of the Qing Dynasty. He had numerous students, among whom Liu Chengyou was the most outstanding.

2. Chen Zizheng

Chen Zizheng (1878-1933), also called Chen Jiping, was from Xiongxian County, Hebei Province. He loved Martial Arts since young and had learned the essence of Shaolin Martial Arts, Overturning Fist, the Yue-style Freehand Fighting, and Eagle Claw Arresting Skills. Chen was diligent and proficient at using the fists, palms, arms, legs, and body. His "claws" were so pointed and fingers so hard that they were able to damage things and hurt one's bones and flesh. He had amazing arm strength and was good at Eagle Claw Fist, so he was reputed as the "King of Eagle Claw Fist". He was the author of *Eagle Claw Overturning Fist*, *Eagle Claw Fist Skills*, *Fifty Ways of Eagle Claw Continuous Fist*, and *A Summary of Eagle Claw Overturning Fist*.

拳这一文化瑰宝，2011年，佛山精武体育会成立鹰爪拳传承发展中心；2012年，曾坤与弟子陈健志、女儿曾秀珠等发起成立佛山市武术协会鹰爪拳会；2015年9月，“佛山鹰爪拳”被列入佛山市第五批非物质文化遗产名录；2016年，佛山市南海区鹰爪拳体育协会、禅城区祖庙街道鹰爪拳会也相继成立。

佛山是目前鹰爪拳的主要衍生地。鹰爪拳经佛山传至广州等地，并辐射到新加坡、马来西亚、文莱、法国、加拿大、澳大利亚等国家，因此佛山成为鹰爪拳南传和外传的重要一站。

（四）鹰爪拳主要套路

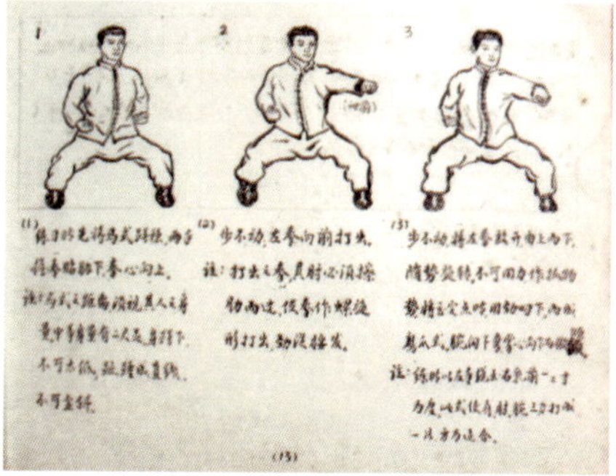

区荣钜研习鹰爪十路行拳的拳谱及笔记

Ou Rongju's boxing manuscript and notes of Ten-Way Walking Fists of Eagle Claw Fist

历史上佛山曾研习过的鹰爪拳套路有徒手拳术，包括鹰爪功、五十路连拳、十路行拳、八步拳、少林捶、太祖拳、八步捶、前八面捶、后八面捶、大绵掌、小绵掌、大雄拳、小雄拳、罗汉拳、雁行拳、四六拳、六合拳、梅花拳、五虎拳、五花豹、前溜势、醉刘唐、一百零八手、对绵掌等；也有器械套路，包括大连环剑、小连环剑、梅花刀、六合刀、连环刀、雪片双刀、梅花双刀、地趟双刀、奇门棍、齐眉棍、连环枪、罗汉枪、梅花枪、六合枪、春秋大刀、四门大刀、单刀对枪、双刀对枪、捕虎枪对拆等。

（五）鹰爪拳名人名师

1. 刘仕俊

刘仕俊（1840—1910），河北雄县孤庄头村人，自幼酷爱练武。后师承法成师傅学习岳氏连拳（后名鹰爪连拳）、三步枪、五步枪、缠枪、串枪、鹞子枪、五路大枪等。他还向道济和尚（法成的师兄）学习鹰爪擒拿术。三年后，刘仕俊辞师云游，并以毕生精力钻研拳艺，传艺授徒，威震四方，因其善使大杆子，被人誉为“大杆子刘”。刘仕俊后又在京城护驾军神机营担任教官，一生有众多弟子，其族孙刘成有为其众多徒弟中的佼佼者。

2. 陈子正

陈子正（1878—1933），又名陈纪平，河北雄县人，自幼好武，得少林拳、翻子拳、岳氏散手、鹰爪擒拿法之精华。陈子正刻苦勤奋，练就多种功法，拳、掌、臂、腿、身处处是功，爪利指坚，抓物物损、抓人则骨肉俱伤。臂力过人，擅长鹰爪拳，被人誉为“鹰爪王”。著有《鹰爪翻子拳》《鹰爪拳艺书》《鹰爪连拳五十路》《鹰爪翻子拳摘要》等书。

3. 刘法孟

刘法孟（1902—1964），河北雄县孤庄头村人，两次南来佛

鹰爪拳
Eagle Claw Fist

3. Liu Fameng

Liu Fameng (1902-1964) was from Guzhuangtou Village, Xiongxian County, Hebei Province. He came to Foshan twice and was an important disseminator of Foshan Eagle Claw Fist. When he was twelve, he learned Eagle Claw Fist from his uncle Liu Qiwen. He was the author of *An Overview of Shaolin Eagle Claw Overturning Fist* and *108 Arresting Skills of Eagle Claw Fist.*

4. Li Peixian

Li Peixian (1892-1985) was originally from Xinhui, Guangdong, whose family lived in Foshan for generations. He loved martial arts and once practiced Hakka Fist in his teens. In 1919, he learned Eagle Claw Fist from Chen Zizheng. After six years' systemic training, he obtained his senior graduation certificate. After the founding of the People's Republic of China, he taught martial arts in Guangzhou. He was good at summing up practical experience and had abundant publications.

Since 2009, Zeng Kun and his students started sorting out historical documents of Foshan Eagle Claw Fist. In 2012, with the initiation of Zeng Kun, Chen Jianzhi, Zeng Xiuzhu and others, Eagle Claw Fist Society of Foshan Martial Arts Association was founded to connect fellow students and to serve as a communication platform. In 2015, Foshan Eagle Claw Fist was included in the List of the Fifth Batch of Foshan Intangible Cultural Heritage, so its inheritance and development in Foshan have been greatly boosted.

山，是佛山鹰爪拳的重要传播者。刘法孟12岁师从叔叔刘启文学习鹰爪拳。著有《少林鹰爪翻子拳术大观》《鹰爪门一百零八擒拿术》等。

4. 李佩弦

李佩弦（1892—1985），祖籍广东新会，世居佛山。喜爱武术，少年时代曾学过客家拳。1919年跟随陈子正学习鹰爪拳，经6年系统训练，获高级毕业证书。中华人民共和国成立后，在广州传授武术。善于总结实践经验，著述甚丰。

2009年起，曾坤与弟子一起着手整理佛山鹰爪拳的历史资料。2012年，曾坤、陈健志、曾秀珠等发起创办佛山市武术协会鹰爪拳会，多方联络同门，积极搭建平台。2015年佛山鹰爪拳被列入佛山市第五批非物质文化遗产名录。如今，鹰爪拳在佛山的传承发展如枯木逢春，焕发出勃勃生机。

第五节　螳螂拳

（一）螳螂拳历史源流

关于螳螂拳产生的年代，目前有三种说法，一说是源于宋代王朗——马成鑫在《螳螂派拳术缘起》一文中载“吾派之鼻祖王朗，宋人也”[1]；另一说是明末清初，同为王朗所创；再一说是清代，创拳者也是王朗[2]。经螳螂门中人查证，王朗是山东栖霞人，姓于名七，曾投少林习艺，一心报效国家。无奈清兵入关，报国无门，便以王朗之名隐迹于崂山。他融合宋、元、明三个朝代十八家法的精华，创出了螳螂拳。

螳螂拳在民间历代流传，至清代乾隆、嘉庆年间为山东莱阳升霄道人所得。升霄道人将螳螂拳传与李之箭（1810—？），李之箭学成后在济南设镖局，以“闪电手”“快手李”等名驰大江南北。李之箭传艺于王云生，后者按门徒的身体素质因材施教，使该拳种

1　马成鑫：《螳螂派拳术缘起》，载《佛山精武月刊》，1928年第2卷第7期。
2　百康：《螳螂拳派拳术之由来》，载《精武画报》，1929年第2卷第8期。

3.5 Mantis Fist

I. History of Mantis Fist

There are three different opinions concerning the time when Mantis Fist was created. One is that it was created by Wang Lang of the Song Dynasty, which was recorded in Ma Chengxin's *Origin of Mantis Fist*, "Wang Lang, the creator of our school of martial arts lived in Song Dynasty" [1]. Another is that it was created by Wang Lang in the late Ming and early Qing dynasties. Still another is that it was created by Wang Lang in the Qing Dynasty [2]. According to the research of its followers, Wang Lang was from Qixia, Shandong Province, whose real name was Yu Qi. He once learned martial arts in Shaolin Temple and was dedicated to serving the country. After the Qing ruler began to take charge of the country, he had no way to realize his aspirations but to live in seclusion in the Laoshan Mountain in Shandong Province under the name Wang Lang. He integrated the essence of 18 different martial arts schools of the Song, Yuan and Ming dynasties to create Mantis Fist.

Mantis Fist was passed on among the folks for generations. When it came to the Qianlong and Jiaqing periods of the Qing Dynasty, it was imparted to the Taoist Monk Shengxiao from Laiyang, Shandong Province. He taught it to Li Zhijian (1810-?). After Li mastered the skills, he established an escort company

1 Ma Chengxin, "Origin of Mantis Fist," *Foshan Jingwu Monthly*, No. 7, Vol. 2, 1928.

2 Bai Kang, "Source of Mantis Fist," *Jingwu Pictorial*, No. 8, Vol. 2, 1929.

in Ji'nan, Shandong and was known in China as "Flash Hands" and "Fast Hand Li". Li passed on Mantis Fist to Wang Yunsheng, who taught students according to their respective physique. Later Mantis Fist developed into the three schools of Seven-Star Mantis Fist, Plum Blossom Mantis Fist and Six-Harmony Mantis Fist.

Fan Xudong, Wang's first student, was the most accomplished in learning Seven-Star Mantis Fist. Fan was a native of Dahaiyang Village, Yantai, Shandong in the late Qing Dynasty. With a fierce martial arts style, Fan was especially good at Iron Palms. At the recommendation of martial artists, Fan went to Siberia, Russian to fight with a Russian of unusual strength and won the competition, thus greatly boosting the reputation of Seven-Star Mantis Fist. Fan's formal students mainly included Guo Jialu, Yang Weixin, Lin Jingshan, Luo Guangyu, and Wang Chuanyi, who carried on his endeavors.

II. Southward spread and development of Mantis Fist

Luo Guangyu, Chen Zizheng of Eagle Claw Fist and Zhao Lianhe of Shaolin Martial Arts were called "the Three Jingwu Masters". Luo had laid a solid foundation for the southward and westward development of Mantis Fist and for its spread to the Malay Archipelago, thus exerting profound influences. The life stories of Luo were recorded in detail in *Origin of Mantis Fist* written by his student Ma Chengxin, "Luo Guangyu is a native of Penglai, Shandong Province. He has a strong build and bright and piercing eyes. He is heroic, majestic, amiable and low-profile. He is a born chivalrous man."

After he was employed by Shanghai Jingwu Sports Association, Luo had trained numerous people and had tremendous influences at home and abroad.

III. Mantis Fist introduced into Foshan

After Foshan Jingwu Sports Association was founded in 1921, martial arts were taught by coaches designated by Shanghai Central Jingwu Sports Association, which in 1923 sent Li Peixian to Foshan Jingwu Sports Association as Director

螳螂拳
Mantis Fist

后来形成了七星螳螂、梅花螳螂、六合螳螂三大流派。

王云生门下习七星螳螂拳较有成就者，是其大弟子范旭东。范旭东是清代末年山东烟台大海阳村人，拳风刚烈，擅长铁砂掌。他曾受武术界人士公推，远赴俄罗斯西伯利亚霍地应战俄国大力士，大胜而归，使七星螳螂拳名声大噪。范旭东入室弟子主要有郭嘉禄、杨维新、林景山、罗光玉、王传义等5人，世传其业。

（二）螳螂拳南传发展

罗光玉与鹰爪派陈子正、少林派赵连和并称为“精武三大名师”。他为螳螂拳由北而南、由东而西以至马来群岛的发展奠定了重要基础，可谓影响深远。关于罗光玉的生平事迹，其弟子马成鑫的《螳螂拳术源流》中记载甚详：“罗光玉，山东蓬莱人也。躯干雄伟，目炯炯有神，豪爽之气溢于眉宇，风骨棱棱，襟怀落落，待人接物蔼然可亲而不着形迹，此盖侠有生以俱来者也。”

罗光玉受聘于上海精武会后，培育人才众多，在海内外影响非凡。

（三）螳螂拳传入佛山

1921年佛山精武会成立后，国术一门由上海精武会选派教员任教。1923年，上海精武会选派李佩弦为佛山精武会国操部主任，李佩弦在上海曾师从罗光玉学习螳螂拳，到佛山任职后，除教授精武

20世纪80年代，李佩弦演示螳螂拳（李家驹供图）

Li Peixian demonstrating Mantis Fist in the 1980s (photo provided by Li Jiaju)

of the National Gymnastics Division. Li once learned Mantis Fist from Luo Guangyu in Shanghai. After his arrival in Foshan, Li started teaching Mantis Fist apart from the basic martial arts of Jingwu Ten Sets.

In view of the great numbers of learners, in order to enhance teaching, in 1927, Foshan Jingwu Sports Association requested more Mantis Fist coaches from Shanghai Jingwu Sports Association. Luo Guangyu sent his student Fan Yongzhen to teach in Foshan. The early members of Foshan Jingwu Sports Association, apart from mastering the Jingwu basic skills, also practiced Mantis Fist. The Association also incorporated the techniques of Mantis Fist in its self-compiled dances.

From the 1950s to the 1990s, with the efforts of Liang Zhensheng, Wei Xihong, and other masters, Seven-Star Mantis Fist won large numbers of followers and became a major martial arts type in Foshan.

In March 2009, Zhong Lianbao, a great Seven-Star Mantis Fist master, following the footsteps of Luo Guangyu, started teaching Seven-Star Mantis Fist in Foshan. His arrival pushed its inheritance and development to a new height.

IV. Major inheritors of Mantis Fist in Foshan

The first generation: Li Zhijian.

The second generation: Wang Yunsheng.

The third generation: Fan Xudong (Fan Xiangsheng) and others.

The fourth generation: Lin Jingshan, Luo Guangyu and others.

The fifth generation:

(1) Lin Jingshan's branch—Zhong Lianbao and others.

(2) Luo Guangyu's branch—Fan Yongzhen and seven others.

The sixth generation:
(1) Fan Yongzhen, Ma Chengxin, Zou Xigong, Yu Lejiang and Chen Zhenyi's branch—Foshan Jingwu Sports Association members.
(2) Liang Zhensheng's branch—Luo Rongqiang (nicknamed "Fish-Seller Qiang") and twelve others.
(3) Li Riqing's branch—Chen Zhiyong and Feng Yaolun.
(4) Zhu Mingsheng's branch—Zhu Yan and eleven others.
(5) Zhong Lianbao's branch—Chen Canming and seven others.
The seventh generation:
(1) Mai Guochi's branch—Wu Zuwei, Wu Zuyao, Li Jiawei and others.
(2) Gu Hongmin's branch—Wang Pufeng, Yu Nong and others.
(3) He Qichi's branch—Tan Zhenjie, Shang Zhongshan and others.
(4) Wei Xihong's branch—Xie Qingtian and 56 others.
(5) Zhu Jiang's branch—Huo Dongyu and 21 others.
(6) Liu Shiqing's branch—Huang Zhixing, Xiao Fan, Mai Haiming and others.
The eighth generation: Chen Canming's branch—Chen Zhongqian and 28 others.

V. Great Mantis Fist master in Foshan

1. Liang Zhensheng

Liang Zhensheng (1910-1973), also named Liang Qiushi, was a native of Lishui, Nanhai and lived at Kuaizi Road in Foshan. He was born in a rich martial arts family, whose ancestors made a living as armed escorts. Liang Zhensheng first learned martial arts from Yu Lejiang, and then from Luo Guangyu at the recommendation of Yu. Later Liang invited Yu to stay at his home and teach him Mantis Fist for a few years. Because of his diligence, Liang finally mastered the essence of Mantis Fist and became a great Mantis Fist master in Foshan.
Liang Zhensheng, not contented with just mastering one type of martial arts, tried to take advantage of and integrate the various schools to cultivate martial arts ethics and to unite different schools, which won him high praise in the martial arts circle. At the beginning of the People's Republic of China, Liang

十套基本拳术外，也传授螳螂拳。

由于从习者众，为了加强螳螂拳的教学，1927年，佛山精武会向上海精武总会延聘螳螂拳专项教员。罗光玉派弟子范永振到佛山任教。早期佛山精武会的会员，除了精通精武基本拳外，也普遍学习了螳螂拳。精武会自编的舞蹈，也将螳螂拳的招式融入其中。

20世纪50—90年代，七星螳螂拳在梁振声、韦锡鸿和其他师傅的努力传承和发扬下，吸引了不少爱好者踊跃学习，成为当时佛山的一大拳种。

2009年3月，七星螳螂拳大师钟连宝追随罗光玉的足迹，开始在佛山传授七星螳螂拳，钟连宝师傅的到来，将佛山七星螳螂拳的传承和发展推向又一个高峰。

（四）螳螂拳在佛山的主要传承脉络

第一代：李之箭。

第二代：王云生。

第三代：范旭东（范翔生）等。

第四代：林景山、罗光玉等。

第五代：（1）林景山支线——钟连宝等。

（2）罗光玉支线——范永振等8人。

第六代：（1）范永振、马成鑫、邹喜功、于乐江、陈振仪支线——佛山精武会众人。

（2）梁振声支线——罗荣强（“卖鱼强”）等13人。

（3）黎日晴支线——陈志勇、冯耀伦。

（4）朱明生支线——朱衍等12人。

（5）钟连宝支线——陈灿明等8人。

第七代：（1）麦国炽支线——吴祖伟、吴祖耀、李嘉维等。

（2）顾洪民支线——王普丰、雨农等。

（3）何其炽支线——谭振杰、尚中山等。

（4）韦锡鸿支线——谢庆添等57人。

（5）朱江支线——霍东宇等22人。

（6）刘世清支线——黄支兴、小范、麦海明等。

第八代：陈灿明支线——陈仲骞等29人。

（五）佛山螳螂拳名师录

1. 梁振声

梁振声（1910—1973），别名球石、虬石，祖籍南海里水，居佛山筷子路。他出身于武术世家，祖辈以走镖为业，家境殷厚。梁振声先为于乐江学生，后经于乐江介绍，拜罗光玉门下为弟子。其后延请于乐江在家奉养多年。梁振声刻苦勤奋，用心钻研，终得螳螂拳拳术真谛，成为佛山螳螂拳一代名师。

梁振声不以一家拳术而自满，他博采众长，兼收并蓄，注重武德修养，团结不同门派，深为武术界同人称道。中华人民共和国成立初期曾任佛山市武术协会主席、武术裁判等职，开办各类武术培训班，为佛山武术体育事业的发展贡献良多。

Zhensheng served as President of Foshan Martial Arts Association and a martial arts referee. He also ran various martial arts training classes, contributing greatly to the development of martial arts in Foshan.

2. Wei Xihong

Wei Xihong, a native of Foshan, learned Seven-Star Mantis Fist from Liang Zhensheng at the age of 17 in the late 1960s. Under the meticulous guidance of Master Liang, Wei learned the essence of the Fist. At the age of 19, he was sent by his teacher to teach martial arts in Taiping, Xiqiao, Nanhai and started to show his talents. He had outstanding skills and was good at real fighting. His movements were fast and firm. His strength was crisp, heavy, thorough, and speedy. In 1986, Wei Xihong helped Huang Yingxin and other older masters to rejuvenate Foshan Jingwu Sports Association.

3. Zhong Lianbao

Zhong Lianbao, a native of Yantai, Shandong Province, has loved martial arts since young. In July 1953, he began to learn Seven-Star Mantis Fist from Lin Jingshan, Fan Xudong's third student. After several decades of painstaking training and studies, he has inherited the style and fighting techniques of Mantis Fist. Now, Zhong has been sparing no efforts to promote and spread Seven-Star Mantis Fist, and excavating, sorting out and developing this precious cultural heritage.

VI. Major routines of Mantis Fist

1. Freehand fighting skills

Freehand fighting skills include Black Tiger Stealing the Heart, Piercing Strikes and Breaking Steps, White Ape Exiting the Cave, White Ape Stealing a Peach, Dodging Hardness, Essentials, Eight-Step Chasing Cicadas, Small Ring Buckles, Hanging Chain Rings, Drunken Mantis, Plum Blossom Falling, Eighteen Hands, Black Tiger Crosses, and Yanqing Eighteen Turns.

2. Sparring skills

Sparring skills include Breaking Steps Sparring, Eighteen Hands Sparring, Lohan Long and Short Beating, Black Tiger Stealing the Heart Sparring, and

螳螂拳

Mantis Fist

2. 韦锡鸿

韦锡鸿，佛山人。20世纪60年代末，17岁的韦锡鸿拜入梁振声门下学习七星螳螂拳。经师父悉心传授，得七星螳螂拳精髓，19岁已受其师委派只身到南海西樵太平开班授拳，崭露头角。他武艺高强，擅长搏击实战，出招速度快且狠，劲力脆、沉、重、透，反应也极快。1986年，韦锡鸿协助黄颖心等老前辈，参与主持重整佛山精武会事务。

3. 钟连宝

钟连宝，山东烟台人，自幼酷爱武术，自1953年7月起拜范旭东第三弟子林景山为师学习七星螳螂拳，经过数十年的刻苦训练和潜心钻研，传承了螳螂拳法风格和技击特色。如今，钟连宝正不遗余力地推广和传播七星螳螂拳，为挖掘整理和发展这份宝贵的民族文化遗产付出艰辛的努力。

（六）螳螂拳主要套路

1. 徒手拳术

有黑虎偷心、插捶崩步、白猿出洞、白

猿偷桃、躲刚、摘要、八步赶蝉、小环扣、揪挂连环、醉螳螂、梅花落、十八手、黑虎交叉、燕青十八翻等。

2. 对练拳术

有崩步对拆、十八手对拆、罗汉长短打、黑虎偷心对练、螳螂短打等。

3. 单练器械

有双匕首、义合七星刀、燕青刀、虎头双勾、扑刀、螳螂剑、青风剑、穿林剑、昆仑剑、游龙剑、猴棍、回环棒、梅花枪、六合枪、九节鞭、三节棍等。

（七）螳螂拳风格特色及技法

螳螂拳的风格特色是刚柔相济，长短相兼，轻而不浮，稳而不滞，刚而不僵，柔而不软，快而不乱，脆而不短。讲究长打短，快打慢，巧胜拙，硬欺软。要求步到拳到，击手必连及步。每式动作都实用，贯穿紧凑，一气呵成。

Mantis Short Fighting.

3. Single-person training weapons

Single-person training weapons include Double Daggers, Yihe Seven-Star Broadswords, Yanqing Swords, Tiger-Head Double Hooks, Long-Handled Swords, Mantis Swords, Clear-Wind Swords, Forest-Crossing Swords, Kunlun Swords, Meandering Dragon Swords, Monkey Clubs, Circle Clubs, Plum Blossom Spears, Six-Harmony Spears, Nine-Section Whips, and Three-Section Clubs.

1959年，罗强演示螳螂拳派六合枪法（罗强供图）

Luo Qiang demonstrating Six-Harmony Spear skills of Mantis Fist in 1959 (photo provided by Luo himself)

VII. Characteristics and techniques of Mantis Fist

Mantis Fist features combination of softness and hardness and of long and short movements and weapons. It is light but not frivolous, steady but not stagnant, hard but not rigid, soft but not weak, fast but not messy, and crisp but not short. It stresses length beating shortness, fastness beating slowness, deftness beating clumsiness and hardness hitting softness. It requires synchronization of the steps and fists. Every movement should be suited to the specific situation and be accomplished in one go.

3.6 Six-Harmony and Eight-Method Fist

I. History of Six-Harmony and Eight-Method Fist

Six-Harmony and Eight-Method Fist (short for Huayue Xinyi Six-Harmony and Eight-Method Fist), is also called Water Fist or Xiantian San Pan Shi Er Shi. It is an ancient Chinese martial arts type whose origin remains unknown and has been passed down by word of mouth. Legend has it that Chen Tuan, a Taoist sage in the Northern Song Dynasty (960-1127) created this martial arts type by integrating Taoist breathing techniques *Tuna* (exhalation and inhalation) and *Daoyin* (a series of body and mind unity exercises) into his own martial arts techniques.

Following Chen Tuan, Li Dongfeng learned Six-Harmony and Eight-Method Fist in a mountain. Later, Li handed it down to Guan Jie and Liu Yunsheng. Afterwards, this martial arts type gained popularity in Shanxi and Henan, with the Five-Character Summary and verses circulated in the crowd. Wang Dewei, a villager of Dawei Village, Xianyang, Shaanxi, became the next successor and changed the name into Water Fist. In addition, Wang taught it to Yuanrong, a Taoist monk, who later modified the form to merge it with his own techniques. Six-Harmony and Eight-Method Fist spread to Sichuan and Shaanxi and was given the name *Yuan Tong* Ba Fa(Flexible Eight Methods). Later, Li Li acquired it and passed it on to Pan Zhihe who then handed it down to Yang Jingqun, Li Chan, Chen Helyu, Shi Dayuan and others.

In the Daoguang period (1821-1850) of the Qing Dynasty, Six-Harmony and Eight-Method Fist was first passed on to Chen Guangdi by Monk Dayuan.

第六节　六合八法拳

（一）六合八法拳历史渊源

六合八法拳，又名水拳，也称先天三盘十二势，全称为华岳心意六合八法拳。这一古老拳种的起源没有确切文献记载，只得民间口传。相传该拳源自北宋年间道家隐士陈抟，他运用武学技艺，结合玄门吐纳、导引之术创编而成。

在陈抟之后，有李东风者隐居山中修炼此法，由他传给关杰和刘韵生二人，此拳在山西、河南流传，有歌诀传世。其后，陕西咸阳大魏村人王德威得承其艺，将六合八法拳改名为“水拳”，并将此拳传给圆融道人，圆融道人融合固有所学，在四川、陕西一带传播该拳，称其为“圆通八法”。继有李梨习得此拳，传授给潘志和，由潘志和传授给杨景群、李蝉、陈鹤侣和释达远等人。

六合八法拳历经辗转，到了清代道光年间，初经佛门中人达远传给了弟子陈光第。陈光第是河北省原昌平县黄花镇人，青年时期在河南开封经商，得遇李蝉道人再习六合八法拳。李蝉道人门下弟子中，有名叫范固国者，是黄河北崖范家滩人，年轻时已身怀绝技而远近闻名。

清光绪二十二年（1896），原籍东北铁岭的吴翼翚拜闫国兴为师，学习韦陀功、三盘十二势、六合八法及长短器械。

吴翼翚转益多师，二十出头已是造诣颇深的武术人才。

清光绪三十一年（1905），吴翼翚考入北洋陆军武备学堂，课余于郊外练习拳术，遇六合八法拳前辈陈鹤侣，得他指授，技艺更加精进，并深谙六合八法拳之真谛。吴翼翚认为：六合八法拳的理论深奥，既有完整的拳学体系，传承千年，又有武当兼少林的古老拳种。[1]

吴翼翚文武兼修，于20世纪20年代先后在河南开封豫萃中学以及上海南方高中、南洋高等商业学校等校担任国文教师和教务主任等职，1932年任上海青年会国术组总指导、六合八法拳总教练。1957年获上海市市长陈毅聘任为上海文史研究馆第一批馆员。1958年3月29日，吴翼翚与世长辞。

（二）六合八法拳传入佛山

六合八法拳传入佛山是在20世纪40年代末期，其第一人为黄佰祥。

黄佰祥（1899—1972），出身于原南海县沙头（丹灶镇小杏

1 庞玉森等：《中央国术馆史》，黄山书社1996年版。“又有”意为“又包含着”。

六合八法拳

Six-Harmony and Eight-Method Fist

Born in Huanghua Town, Changping County, Hebei Province, Chen was a businessman in Kaifeng, Henan in his youth. After he met Li Chan, a Taoist monk, Chen started learning Six-Harmony and Eight-Method Fist. Among his students, one was called Fan Guguo, a native of Fanjiatan in the north bank of the Yellow River. When young, Fan was already well-known practice for his superb martial arts techniques.

In the 22nd year of the Guangxu period (1896) of the Qing Dynasty, Wu Yihui, a native of Tieling in Northeast China, learned martial arts such as Weituo Skills, Three Levels of Practice and Twelve Animation Tendencies, Six-Harmony and Eight-Method Fist as well as long and short weapons from Yan Guoxing.

Under the tutelage of multiple masters, Wu became an accomplished martial arts master in his early twenties.

In the 31st year of the Guangxu period (1905), Wu was admitted to Beiyang Military Academy. While practicing martial arts after class in the suburbs, he met Chen Helyu, a Six-Harmony and Eight-Method Fist master, who enlightened him, so Wu tremendously improved his Six-Harmony and Eight-Method Fist skills and acquired its quintessence. In Wu's opinion, Six-Harmony and Eight-Method Fist is a profound martial arts type with a comprehensive system and over a thousand years of history; and it has borrowed some skills from Shaolin and Wudang schools. [1]

Wu Yihui was good at both arts and arms. In the 1920s, he worked in several schools as a Chinese teacher and Dean of Studies, including in Kaifeng Yucui Middle School, Shanghai South Senior High School, and Shanghai Nanyang High School. In 1932, he became the general instructor of martial arts and head coach of Six-Harmony and Eight-Method Fist at Shanghai Youth Association. In 1957, he was appointed by Mayor Chen Yi as one of the first librarians of Shanghai Research Institute of Culture and History. He passed away on March 29, 1958.

1 Pang Yusen, et al, *History of the Central Martial Arts Institute*. Hefei: Huangshan Publishing House, 1996.

六合八法拳

Six-Harmony and Eight-Method Fist

II. Six-Harmony and Eight-Method Fist introduced into Foshan

Six-Harmony and Eight-Method Fist was introduced into Foshan in the late 1940s by Huang Baixiang.

Huang (1899-1972), was born in a wealthy family of academics in Shatou, the former Nanhai County (now Xiaoxing Village, Danzao Town, Nanhai District), and started to learn Six-Harmony and Eight-Method Fist from Liang Zipeng, his senior fellow student, after the victory of the War of Resistance against Japanese Aggression.

In 1949, Huang performed Six-Harmony and Eight-Method Fist during a celebration at the invitation of Li Peixian of Foshan Jingwu Sports Association, which was an eye-opener to the peer martial arts practitioners. At the end of the celebration, Huang was asked to stay in Foshan to teach Six-Harmony and Eight-Method Fist. As a result, Huang became the first to teach it in Foshan at the invitation of Ou Rongju, Pan Yanliu, Ren Wenshi, Zeng Gen, Mai Yichou and Feng Chuyi.

In 1952, Huang left Foshan for his hometown in Shatou, Nanhai and continued teaching Six-Harmony and Eight-Method Fist. His son Huang Qitai inherited his skills and his students in Foshan, such as Ou Rongju and Zeng Gen, also inherited and developed the martial arts type well.

III. New development of Six-Harmony and Eight-Method Fist in Foshan

In 1994, new dynamism was injected into Foshan's Six-Harmony and Eight-Method Fist as Lu Guiyao, a formal student of Wu Yihui's, came back to Foshan after retirement to teach Six-Harmony and Eight-Method Fist. In 2004, at the initiative of Lu, Six-Harmony and Eight-Method Fist Committee of Foshan Martial Arts Association was established, enabling this martial arts type to further develop and flourish alongside other schools of martial arts in Foshan.

村）的书香门第，家境殷实。抗日战争胜利后，从师兄梁子鹏深造六合八法拳。

20世纪80年代，区荣钜演示六合八法拳（区荣钜供图）
Ou Rongju demonstrating Six-Harmony and Eight-Method Fist in the 1980s (photo provided by Ou himself)

1949年，黄佰祥应佛山精武体育会李佩弦邀请参加庆典活动，即兴表演了六合八法拳，使佛山精武同人眼界大开。活动结束后，大家都希望黄佰祥能留驻佛山教授六合八法拳。黄佰祥因此应佛山区荣钜、潘炎流、任文石、曾根、麦益侍、冯雏仪等邀请，成为在佛山传授六合八法拳的第一人。

1952年，黄佰祥离开佛山回到家乡南海沙头，继续传授六合八法拳，其子黄启泰承其衣钵，而他的佛山门徒如区荣钜、曾根等也将六合八法拳传承发扬。

（三）国术薪传发新枝

1994年，在佛山传承已久的六合八法拳又注入了新的力量——吴翼翚的入室弟子卢桂耀回到佛山安度晚年，在佛山传授六合八法拳。2004年，在卢桂耀的发起下，“佛山市武术协会六合八法拳术专业委员会”成立，六合八法拳这一拳种在佛山武术百花园中深深扎根，枝繁叶茂。

第七节　周家拳

（一）周家拳历史渊源

周家拳是清末民初广东新会人周龙将所学洪拳、蔡家拳和北少林拳融合而成的一种独特拳术、器械的总称。周龙创拳后，先传授给周家兄弟，他与他的4位弟弟周协、周彪、周海、周田并称“周家五虎”。二十世纪二三十年代，该拳种曾独步岭南，流传广远，声名鼎盛；二十世纪三十年代后传至海外，周家因此拳而世称“中外周家”。

周家拳创始人周龙清光绪十七年（1891）生于广东省新会县棠下镇沙富村观莲里（今广东省江门市蓬江区辖管），受洪拳于周雄，并从肇庆高要人蔡九公受蔡家拳法。

传人有南海九江邓波棠、关辉洪、潘永生，顺德杏坛陈兆辉，新会周家拳五虎纪念馆馆长周宝洪，等等。

3.7 Zhou Jia Quan

I. History of Zhou Jia Quan

Zhou Jia Quan is a general term for a unique form of freehand fighting and weapons created by Zhou Long, a native of Xinhui, Guangdong Province in the late Qing Dynasty and the early Republic of China by combining Hong Quan, Cai Jia Quan and the Northern Shaolin Fist. After Zhou Long's creation, he passed it on to his four younger brothers, Zhou Xie, Zhou Biao, Zhou Hai, and Zhou Tian. They were collectively called the "Five Tigers of the Zhou Family". In the 1920s and 1930s, the martial arts type spread widely in Lingnan and enjoyed great reputation. After the 1930s, it spread overseas and the Zhou family was thus called "the Zhou Family in China and Overseas".

周彪练拳照
Zhou Biao practicing martial arts

Zhou Long, the creator of Zhou Jia Quan, was born in 1891 at Guanlianli, Shafu Village, Tangxia Town, Xinhui

周家拳
Zhou Jia Quan

（二）藤牌层层叠，狮艺显奇功

1924年1月20日，孙中山在广州主持召开中国国民党第一次全国代表大会，据闻，当时广州全市50多间武馆参与舞狮游行庆祝，大小商铺纷纷挂青[1]助庆，周家拳馆因藤牌叠加、轻功采青而威名远播。

（三）周家拳在佛山流传

二十世纪二三十年代，周家拳在以周龙为首的“周家五虎”拳师带领下以广州为中心向周边城乡传播发展。民国15年（1926），周家拳馆设第十六、十七分馆于顺德县陈村和佛山。

民国时期，周家拳已在佛山及周边城镇、乡村传播。目前，在佛山市南海区，有狮山镇周馆、九江“英勇堂”上东武术龙狮体育会、九江“振兴”武术馆；在顺德区，有里海南溪醒狮团、杏坛周琪兴武术纪念馆、杏坛“雄义堂”国术馆；在高明区，有塘花村仁义体育会、罗丹仁义堂体育会，等等。

（四）周家拳拳械套路

1. 徒手拳术

有小伏虎、小洪拳、大洪拳、万字拳、柴桩、大伏虎、虎豹

1　广东民俗，主家挂青，狮子见青即采。

邓波棠演示周家拳（高宇峰供图）
Deng Botang demonstrating Zhou Jia Quan (photo provided by Gao Yufeng)

拳、小四平拳、小四形八卦拳、国字拳、十字拳、五形拳、六角拳、独臂拳、大跛拳、鹰爪拳、花拳、五虎拳。

2. 器械

有双头棍、梅花双刀、十字梅花单刀、十字梅花锁喉枪、八卦棍、九子连环刀、公孙棒、鼠尾棍、双夹单棍、七节单双鞭、九节单双鞭、匕首（又叫插仔）、高凳、十字梅花棍、长烟斗、扁担、禅杖、大耙、锄头、蔡阳刀、双头花枪、蛇矛枪、三节棍等。

3. 对拆套路

有周家伏虎拳对拆，双头棍对拆，双刀拆缨枪，匕首、双筒、

County, Guangdong Province, which is now under the jurisdiction of Pengjiang District, Jiangmen City, Guangdong Province. He learned Hong Quan from Zhou Xiong and Cai Jia Quan from Cai Jiugong of Gaoyao, Zhaoqing.

His successors include Deng Botang, Guan Huihong and Pan Yongsheng of Jiujiang, Nanhai; Chen Zhaohui of Xingtan, Shunde; and Zhou Baohong, Curator of the Memorial Hall of the Five Tigers of the Zhou Family in Xinhui.

II. Stacked-up rattan shields showing remarkable lion dancing skills

On January 20th, 1924, Dr. Sun Yat-sen hosted the first National Congress of the Kuomintang in Guangzhou. It is said that over 50 martial arts gymnasiums took part in the lion dancing parade while all shops, big and small, hung up greens to boost the atmosphere [1]. Zhou Jia Quan Gymnasium made its reputation by stacking up rattan shields to collect the greens with acrobatic skills.

III. Dissemination of Zhou Jia Quan in Foshan

In the 1920s and 1930s, Zhou Jia Quan, under the guidance of the "Five Tigers of the Zhou Family" with Zhou Long as the head, spread to nearby cities and villages with Guangzhou as the center. In 1926, Zhou Jia Quan Gymnasium established its 16th and 17th branches in Chencun Village, the former Shunde County and in Foshan respectively.

During the Republic of China, Zhou Jia Quan was already disseminated in Foshan and its surrounding towns and villages. In Nanhai District of Foshan, there are Zhou Gymnasium in Shishan Town, "Bravery Hall" Martial Arts and Dragon Lion Sports Association in Shangdong Jiujiang, and "Zhenxing" Martial Arts Gymnasium in Jiujiang; in Shunde District, Lihai Nanxi Lion Troupe, Xingtan Zhou Qixing Martial Arts Memorial Hall, and Xingtan "Xiongyi (Righteousness) Hall" Martial Arts Gymnasium; and in Gaoming District,

1 A Cantonese folk custom. The host hangs up greens to be collected by the lions.

Renyi (Benevolence) Sports Association at Tanghua Village and Luodan Renyi (Benevolence) Sports Association.

IV. Freehand fighting and weapon routines of Zhou Jia Quan

1. Freehand fighting skills

Small Tiger Subduing Fists, Small Hong Fists, Big Hong Fists, *Wanzi Fists* (whose movements resemble the Chinese character " 万 "); Wooden Stakes, Big Tiger Subduing Fists, Tiger and Leopard Fists, Small Four-Level Fists, Small Four-Shape *Bagua* Fists, *Guozi* Fists (whose movements resemble the Chinese character " 国 "), Cross Fists, Five-Shape Fists, Hexagon Fists, Single Arm Fists, Big Limp Fists, Eagle Claw Fists, Flower Fists and Five-Tiger Fists.

2. Weapons

Double-Headed Sticks, Plum Blossom Double Swords, Cross Plum Blossom Single Swords, Cross Plum Blossom Throat-Locking Spears, *Bagua* Sticks, Nine Sons Serial Swords, Gongsun Sticks, Mouse-Tail Clubs, Double-Clapped Single Clubs, Seven-Section Single and Double Whips, Nine-Section Single and Double Whips, Daggers, High Stools, Cross Plum Blossom Clubs, Long Smoking Pipes, Shoulder Poles, Monk Canes, Big Rakes, Hoes, Caiyang Swords, Double-Headed Flower Spears, Snake Spears and Three-Section Sticks.

3. Sparring routines

Sparring routines include Zhou Tiger Subduing Sparring, Double-Headed Stick Sparring, Double Swords versus Tasseled Spears, Sparring among Daggers, Double Tubes and Tasseled Spears, Freehand versus Broadswords, *Bagua* Stick Sparring, Three-Section Sticks versus Tasseled Spears, and High Stools versus Hoes.

4. Skill training

Skill training includes hitting three-star stakes and sandbags, which trains different parts of the body including the fists, palms, fingers, knees, feet and heels; exercises such as single pillar stakes, poking at sand, lifting stone barbells, double fists, ten-finger push-ups, four-level horse stakes, standing on one foot, throwing sandbags, snatching wine jars, line-up hitting and *Dantian qi* (vital

周家拳
Zhou Jia Quan

缨枪三人对拆，空手拆刀，八卦棍对拆，三节棍拆缨枪，高凳拆锄头，等等。

4. 功力训练

有打三星桩、打沙包等锻炼拳、掌、指、膝、脚、踭等身体各部位的训练，也有单柱桩、插沙、举石担、双拳、十指头俯卧撑、四平马桩、独立脚、抛沙包功、抓酒缸、排打、丹田气等练习，还有横吊桩、木人桩、棍桩、刀桩等练习。

目前，国内有50多家周家拳会馆，在马来西亚等国家也有周家拳分会馆的身影，学习周家拳者已近万人。为了将沉寂的周家拳唤醒，新加坡华侨商人林振钦带头捐资，在江门市新会区修建了周家拳五虎纪念馆。

energy) exercises. In addition, there is also training with horizontally hung stakes, wooden dummies, stick stakes and sword stakes.

At present, there are over 50 Zhou Jia Quan gymnasiums in China and some branches in other countries such as Malaysia, with a total of nearly 10,000 learners. In order to revitalize Zhou Jia Quan, Lin Zhenqin, a Chinese Singaporean businessman has taken the lead in donating money to build the Memorial Hall of the Five Tigers of the Zhou Family in Xinhui District, Jiangmen City.

FOSHAN, CHINA

第四章 中华人民共和国成立后传入佛山的传统武术

Chapter 4 Traditional Martial Arts Introduced into Foshan after the Founding of the PRC

中华人民共和国成立以后，佛山传统武术依然在传承和发展。其间，传入佛山的主要拳术有龙形拳、白眉拳两种，各有发展，流传并影响至今。其中尤以龙形拳为盛，白眉拳当今亦有传承。

Since the founding of the People's Republic of China in 1949, traditional martial arts have continued to develop in Foshan. Dragon Style Fist and White Eyebrow Fist are the two major types introduced into Foshan during this period. Each has developed in its own way and is still influential today. By comparison, the former is more popular.

4.1 Dragon Style Fist

Dragon Style Fist is a traditional southern martial arts type that is guided by intention and combined with offense and defense. It features sunken heels and drooping arms; energy gathered at *Dantian*; tips of nose, fingers and toes on a vertical plane; and interconnection of the three forces. It was invented in the 1920s by Lin Yaogui by integrating Canton Hakka Fist and Southern Shaolin Martial Arts.

I. History of Dragon Style Fist

Concerning the formation of Dragon Style Fist, there is a couplet handed down from the founder Lin Yaogui: (I) first gained proficiency in Haifeng; then attained authentic skills at Huashou Temple.

Lin Yaogui (1874-1965) was a talented person born in Putou Village, Rengtu Town (now part of Ruhu Town), Boluo County, Guangdong Province. Since his childhood, he started to learn martial arts from his father Lin Qingyuan, who was a student of Huang Lianjiao from the former Haifeng County; and was once instructed by the seniors Master Lin He and Master Lin E. He was agile, tall and strong, diligent and meticulous in learning martial arts. In his early years, Lin Yaogui, following his father, practiced medicine and martial arts in Guishan County (renamed Huiyang County later in 1923) and other places in the Dongjiang River valley, gaining considerable reputation.

In 1896 at Huashou Temple, Lin Yaogui not only mastered martial arts but also inherited the authentic orthopedic skills. That's the source of the couplet.

In 1924 when Huangpu Military Academy was founded, Lin Yaogui was

第一节　龙形拳

龙形拳是以意导引、攻守合一、沉踭落膊、气沉丹田、三尖相对、三力相通的传统南派拳术，20世纪20年代由林耀桂融合广东客家拳及南传少林拳术始创。

（一）龙形拳历史渊源

关于龙形拳的形成，宗师林耀桂传有一联：先学海丰成茂业，后从华首得真传。

林耀桂（1874—1965），出生于广东省博罗县仍图镇（今并入汝湖镇）埔头村，天资聪颖，从小就随父林庆元（曾师从海丰黄连娇）学得武艺，也获祖辈林合、林俄两位老师指导。他刻苦勤奋，功夫扎实，身手敏健，体格魁梧。清代同治年间，林耀桂跟随父亲在归善县（1923年改为惠阳县）及东江流域一带行医习武，名声显赫。

1896年，在华首台，林耀桂不但学得武功，更获跌打医术真传。此为“先学海丰成茂业，后从华首得真传”的来源。

1924年，黄埔军校成立，时任粤军第四军训练部少将的李济深

龙形拳
Dragon Style Fist

appointed as the martial arts drillmaster of the guard camp and the training regiment in the military by Li Jishen, the then Major General of the Training Department of the Fourth Army of Guangdong Military Force.

In September 1926 when Chen Jitang started to head the Guangdong Provincial Government, he reorganized Martial Arts Gymnasium of Guangdong and Guangxi to form Guangzhou Martial Arts Association and continued to appoint Lin Yaogui as the chief instructor.

林耀桂演示龙形拳之攦劈（曾根供图）

The "Splitting" technique of Dragon Style Fist by Lin Yaogui (photo provided by Zeng Gen)

In 1931, Chen Jitang established the Guangdong Military and Political School (also known as Yantang Military School) at Yantang, Guangzhou, and appointed Lin Yaogui as the Colonel Drillmaster. After knowing Lin's experience of learning martial arts and that he didn't belong to any formal school, Chen suggested setting up a "Dragon Style School", which means "robust as a flying dragon and agile as a fierce tiger". He also inscribed the words "Showing modesty doesn't mean weakness. Remain disciplined despite others' strength", as a gift to Lin. As a result, Dragon Style Fist began to develop into an independent martial arts type.

During the War of Resistance against Japanese Aggression, Lin Yaogui compiled the "Maneuvers of Using Broadwords to Combat Japanese Invaders" for officers and soldiers of the Nineteenth Route Army, contributing greatly to fighting against the invaders.

In 1947, the article entitled "Heroes at Fighting Assemblies" carried by *Kwok Wah Daily News* in Guangzhou said that Lin Yaogui had taught tens of thousands of students over the years and that he claimed to have no rivals in Hong Kong and Guangdong".

II. Dissemination of Dragon Style Fist in Foshan

Two brilliant students of Lin Yaogui's developed Dragon Style Fist respectively after it was introduced into Foshan. Ma Qi advanced it in Sanshui, Foshan, while Zeng Gen in the old town of Foshan.

1. The Ma's branch of Dragon Style Fist

In 1998, Zhang Yaoting, President of Chinese Wushu Association, inscribed "Martial Arts Family" for Ma Qi's family.

Ma Qi (1916—2007) was from Shuikeng Village, Zeshan Community, Jingkou Town, Sanshui District, Foshan City. In 1936, he became a student of Lin Yaogui's and learned Dragon Style Fist from him in the second branch of South China Martial Arts Club. In 1947, Ma Qi went back to his hometown, and took it as an opportunity to impart skills of Dragon Style Fist and lion dancing to villagers and set up Dongxinghe Fitness Club [1]. After Lin Yaogui settled in Hong Kong in 1956, Ma Qi began teaching students in Nanhai, Huadu and Qingyuan, as well as in Guangzhou and his hometown Sanshui. In 1988, he founded Guangzhou Dragon Style Fist Association and became its president. In 1989, he set up Ma Qi Dragon Style Fist Gymnasium in his hometown Jingkou. Highly skilled at Dragon Style Fist, Ma Qi had students all over the world and had been an important disseminator in Foshan.

2. Dragon Style Fist in the old town of Foshan

Zeng Gen was regarded as "the father of Foshan Dragon Style Fist" by followers of Foshan Dragon Style Fist.

Zeng Gen (1922-2011) was born in Foshan. In 1950, he went to work in Guangzhou, and became a student of Lin Yaogui's in the latter's twilight years, thanks to the introduction by Li Peixian.

In 1960, Zeng Gen started to teach Dragon Style Fist in Foshan, making it one of the popular martial arts types at that time. His students Luo Qiang, Li Tang,

1 Though Dragon Style Fist was already taught by Ma Qi in 1947, its popularity in Foshan was mainly after 1949. That's why it is still considered a martial arts type introduced into Foshan after the founding of the PRC .

延聘林耀桂为军中护士营、教导团的国术教官。

1926年9月，陈济棠主政广东，将两广国术馆改组为广州国术协会，续聘林耀桂为主任教官。

1931年，陈济棠在广州燕塘成立广东军事政治学校（燕塘军校），延聘林耀桂为上校教官。陈济棠得知林耀桂的学武经历而且无正式派别后，建议定名为“龙形派”，取意“矫若游龙，捷如猛虎”之意，并亲笔题赠“克己让人非我弱，存心守道任他强”。从此，龙形拳开宗立派。

抗战期间，林耀桂曾编“抗日杀敌大刀术”教予十九路军官兵，为抗击侵华日军做出贡献。

1947年广州《国华报》载《搏斗大会英雄谱》一文说林耀桂“历年授徒，数以万计，自谓港、粤二地，未逢敌手”。

（二）龙形拳在佛山传播

龙形拳传入佛山后，林耀桂两名高足分为两脉发展，一是马齐一脉，在三水发展；一是曾根一脉，在佛山老城发展。

1. 龙形拳马家军

1998年，中国武术协会主席张耀庭为马齐一家亲笔题词“武术世家”。

马齐（1916—2007），佛山市三水区迳口择善水坑村人，1936年拜入林耀桂门下，在华南国术社第二支部随师研习龙形拳。1947

马齐带领儿子马国辉和孙子马世勇、马世焰、马世平演练龙形拳（马国辉供图）
Ma Qi, his son Ma Guohui and his grandsons Ma Shiyong, Ma Shiyan and Ma Shiping practicing Dragon Style Fist (photo provided by Ma Guohui)

年，马齐开始利用回乡机会，教授村民龙形拳和醒狮技艺[1]，并在家乡水坑村成立“东星和健身会”。1956年，林耀桂赴港定居后，马齐除在广州、三水家乡授拳外，还在南海、花都、清远等地收徒传艺。他于1988年发起创办广州市龙形拳会，并任会长；1989年在家乡三水迳口创办马齐龙形拳馆。马齐练得一身精湛的龙形拳技艺，徒弟遍布世界各地，是龙形拳在佛山的重要传播者。

2. 龙形拳在佛山老城

佛山龙形拳门人称曾根为“佛山龙形之父”。

曾根（1922—2011）出生于佛山，1950年到广州工作，由李佩

1 虽1947年马齐已在佛山传授龙形拳，但龙形拳在佛山正式广为传播，主要为1949年后事，因此依然大概视龙形拳为中华人民共和国成立后传入佛山的拳种。

龙形拳

Dragon Style Fist

Peng Jiang, Lai Run, Yuan Zhuo, He Yong, Cen Jiexiong, He Jiacheng and He Huanshen as well as their students have played an important role in promoting Dragon Style Fist in Foshan.

In 2006, Zeng Gen advocated to establish Dragon Style Fist Society under Foshan Martial Arts Association, which aimed at binding successors to Dragon Style Fist at home and abroad together through martial arts. He attached great importance to collecting and sorting out traditional martial arts data. He carefully recorded important martial arts routines in the form of pictures and texts. For instance, the martial arts notes taken in his young age, together with the martial arts manuals recording the flat punches and knocks of Cai Li Fo Quan taught by Tang Dongchen and Maneuver Bridges of Dragon Style Fist taught by Lin Yaogui have all become treasures for scholars to study traditional martial arts in Foshan.

III. Major freehand fighting and weapon routines and important tips of Dragon Style Fist

Important tips of offense and defense: (1) attack when you see a flaw and wait otherwise; if you miss it, you will have no chance to strike; (2) defend with your hands against relentless attacks; hit his acupoints sideways against intense attacks; (3) fight back sideways against a straight attack; fight back straight against a sideway attack; do not hastily catch an iron-hard broken "bridge", and defeat it with a smashed "bridge".

1. Freehand fighting

Freehand fighting includes Dragon Style Maneuver Bridges, and Flower Fist Small Horse Stance.

2. Weapon routines

Weapon routines include Single Broadswords, Double Broadswords, Yellow Dragon Sabers, Green Dragon Swords, Two-Section Clubs, Soft Whips, Tasseled Spears, Rakes, Benches, Hoes, Dragon-Shaped Sticks (Yellow Dragon Heart-Piercing Sticks) and so forth.

弦引荐拜入龙形拳宗师林耀桂门下，成为林耀桂晚年弟子。

曾根1960年开始在佛山传授龙形拳，使龙形拳成为当时的热门拳种之一。他门下弟子罗强、利棠、彭江、赖润、袁焯、何永、岑杰雄、何嘉诚、何焕燊等人及其再传弟子，为佛山龙形拳的传播推广发挥了重要的作用。

2006年，曾根倡建佛山市武术协会龙形拳总会，以武术为纽带凝聚海内外龙形拳传人。他十分重视对传统武术资料的收集、整理，对所学的重要拳术套路以图文形式认真记录。他年轻时期的武术笔记，以及其记录的唐栋臣所授的蔡李佛拳之平拳、扣打和林耀桂所授的龙形拳摩桥等拳谱，成为当今研究佛山传统武术的瑰宝。

（三）龙形拳主要拳械套路及要诀

龙形拳的攻防要诀：（1）有空打空，无空收空，有空唔打（不打），何时用劲。（2）他人来得狠，双手要防紧；他人来得烈，横踭来打穴。（3）横来直破，直来横攻，破桥硬如铁，切勿轻易接，用碎桥破之。

1. 徒手拳术

有龙形摩桥、花拳小马。

2. 器械套路

有单刀、双刀、黄龙剑、青龙刀、双节棍、软鞭、缨枪、大耙、横头凳、锄头、龙形穿心棍（黄龙穿心棍）等。

（四）龙形拳技术风格

龙形拳传人霍荣对该拳种的拳理有较深的理解。他在《论龙形拳之功劲》一文中载：功劲为拳法之根，犹如弦上之箭。门派功架、功法是弓，功力为弦，劲力是箭，技法是镞。强弓硬弩出快箭。功夫到家，自然得心应手。龙形摩桥的劲发于桩势，功法在摆桩、扭马、迫步。其摆桩、扭马、迫步讲求气势，吞吐分明，内外五行合一。内练精、气、神，外练腰、桥、马的龙形拳入门功夫，也是龙形拳有别于其他门派的特色之一和掌握、发挥龙形拳威力的精要所在。

（五）佛山龙形拳传承现状

龙形拳传入佛山70多年，门下弟子广泛传播设立多个组织和拳馆。不但在国内广为流传，如在香港设有龙形体育总会，而且走出国门，如在美国、加拿大、英国、法国等国均设有龙形分会，呈蓬勃发展之势。以下为佛山龙形拳各组织机构（按建立时间先后排序）：三水迳口马齐龙形拳馆和拳会，佛山精武体育会龙形拳活动中心，佛山市武术协会龙形拳总会、龙形文龙拳馆、白龙拳馆、东方曾根龙形拳会、龙腾武术体育会、禅龙武术会。

IV. Technical styles of Dragon Style Fist

Huo Rong, an inheritor of Dragon Style Fist, has a deep understanding of the theory. Huo Rong's book, *On the Skills and Strength of Dragon Style Fist*, includes the following content. Skills and strength are essential in Martial Arts, like a bowstring and an arrow. The poses are like a bow; skills a bowstring; strength an arrow; methods an arrowhead. A powerful bow makes a fast arrow. One can practice with high proficiency once he achieves high levels of skills and strength. The strength of Dragon Style Maneuver Bridges originates in the pose, which includes stances, twists and steps. Practicing them requires a strong imposing manner and clear movements, and the integration of the five internal and external shapes. Practicing the strength and basic skills of essence, energy and spirit inside and the waist, bridge hands and horse stances is one of the distinguishing characteristics of Dragon Style Fist from other schools of martial arts, and is the key to mastering and exerting the power of this martial arts type.

V. The status quo of inheritance of Foshan Dragon Style Fist

It has been over 70 years since Dragon Style Fist was introduced into Foshan. It has been widely promoted by its successors, and many organizations and clubs have been set up. It is popular not only in China but also overseas. The Dragon Style Sports Association is headquartered in Hong Kong, with branches in the US, Canada, Britain, France and other countries. The following are organizations of Foshan Dragon Style Fist (in the order of time of establishment): Ma Qi Dragon Style Fist Gymnasium and Association in Jingkou of Sanshui, Dragon Style Fist Center under Foshan Jingwu Sports Association, Dragon Style Fist Society under Foshan Martial Arts Association, Wen Long Dragon Style Fist Club, White Dragon Fist Club, Eastern Zeng Gen Dragon Style Fist Association, Long Teng Martial Arts Sports Association and Chan Long Martial Arts Association.

第二节　白眉拳

（一）白眉拳历史渊源

相传，白眉拳发祥于河南省嵩山少林寺，开宗于四川峨眉山，祖师是明末清初的僧人白眉上人，此派武术最初只流传于庙宇内，未有外传，后白眉上人亲传广慧禅师，广慧禅师将其传至竺法云禅师，至20世纪初，由俗家弟子张礼泉传播于佛门之外。

白眉拳宗师张礼泉
White Eyebrow Fist master Zhang Liquan

张礼泉（1884—1964），字励存，原籍广东省惠阳县（今广东省惠州市内），出生于惠州桥东一个小商人家庭，7岁习武，先后随东江一带的林石、李朦及林合等名师学武。1903年到光孝寺拜竺法云为师，学艺3年，得

4.2 White Eyebrow Fist

I. History of White Eyebrow Fist

White Eyebrow Fist originated from Songshan Shaolin Temple in Henan Province but was established in Mount Emei in Sichuan. The founder was Monk White Eyebrow in the late Ming and early Qing dynasties. At the beginning it was only taught within temples. Monk White Eyebrow passed it on to Zen Master Guanghui, who then imparted it to Zen Master Zhu Fayun. In the early 20th century, the secular disciple Zhang Liquan disseminated it outside temples.

Zhang Liquan (1884-1964), also called Zhang Licun, was a native of Huiyang County (now in Huizhou City), Guangdong Province. He was born into a petty merchant family at Qiaodong, Huizhou. He started practicing martial arts at the age of seven. He had successively followed great masters like Lin Shi, Li Meng and Lin He. In 1903, he went to Guangxiao Temple in Guangzhou to be a student of Zen Master Zhu Fayun's. After three years, he mastered all the skills. Later on the basis of the original moves, he renovated the internal skills and principles of martial arts taught by Zhu Fayun by carefully absorbing the advantages of the different types of martial arts he had learned in earlier years. In 1949, he moved to Hong Kong and in 1964 died of illness at Kowlong, Hong Kong at the age of 80. Zhang Liquan was a great master of White Eyebrow Fist who had integrated different schools. Apart from his sons, he had about 40 students such as Zeng Bohui, Ge Zhaohuang, Chen Guohua, and Xia Hanxiong. With the efforts of Zhang Liquan and his students, White Eyebrow Fist has mainly spread in Guangdong, Hong Kong, Macao, Southeast Asia and North

白眉拳
White Eyebrow Fist

其衣钵真传。其后，他对早期习练的几家拳法进行了精选，在保留原有招式的基础上，对竺法云所授拳术的内功心法和原理进行了改良。1949年，他移居香港，1964年在香港九龙病逝，享年80岁。张礼泉是白眉拳之集大成者，除传授儿子外，门下弟子有曾博惠、葛肇煌、陈国华、夏汉雄等约40人。

白眉拳在张礼泉及其门人的努力下，主要在我国粤、港、澳及东南亚、北美一带流传，并辐射至世界各地。

（二）白眉拳在佛山的传承与发展

白眉拳是南拳中独树一帜的著名拳种，20世纪50年代后期开始传入佛山，20世纪70年代发展到高峰期，从习人员众多。在白眉拳的传播过程中，有两个人物是佛山人最为熟悉的。

1. 仇太生——白眉拳传入佛山第一人

仇太生（1918—1979），广东高明西安崇北村人，自幼爱好武术，16岁后跟随堂叔仇乌学习白眉拳。其后，仇乌推荐其在自己的师傅夏汉雄门下深造白眉拳和跌打医术，之后仇太生的武术和医术都有了更深造诣。

中华人民共和国成立初期，仇太生举家移居佛山。初在李子斌、黄精医馆（今福贤路89号）坐馆行医，夜间小范围教拳帮补家用。20世纪60年代中后期，与刘少良接触最多，交情最深。仇太生的白眉拳艺除传授儿子仇德基外，还授予吕扬照、朱才兴、廖智一、李荫祥、冯永强、陈三、剃头明、陈秋、梁裕熹、徐文正、欧念中等。

2. 刘少良——佛山白眉拳推动播种者

刘少良（1905—1977），祖籍原南海县丹灶沙水，居佛山。早年曾在阳山、连县工作，其间师从竺缘道长（生平不详）学得白眉拳上乘功夫。1963年，刘少良在广州机床厂病退回佛山，后致力于推广和传授白眉拳。他与同门仇太生为挚友，经常共同研讨白眉拳法。

1973年，刘少良传授白眉拳
Liu Shaoliang teaching White Eyebrow Fist in 1973

二十世纪六七十年代是佛山白眉拳发展的繁荣时期。活跃于武坛，卓有成效的推动传统武术的传承发展者，多为刘少良门下弟子。

（三）佛山白眉拳主要组织

白眉拳在佛山历经半个世纪的传播，习练者数以万计，成为佛山武术的重要组成部分，几个主要的传播组织先后成立。

1999年11月3日，佛山精武会白眉拳武术馆成立，馆址位于佛山市新堤路，佛山白眉拳的传授自此有了一个专门的训练基地。2003年5月1日，佛山刘少良武术纪念馆成立，馆址位于佛山市石

America and other places around the world.

II. Inheritance and development of White Eyebrow Fist in Foshan

White Eyebrow Fist is a unique Southern martial arts type. It was introduced into Foshan in the 1950s. In its peak in the 1970s, it was practiced by huge numbers of people. During its dissemination, two people are most familiar to Foshan people.

1. Qiu Taisheng, the first person to introduce White Eyebrow Fist into Foshan

Qiu Taisheng (1918-1979) was from Chongbei Village, Xi'an, Gaoming, Guangdong. He loved martial arts since young. At the age of 16, he learned White Eyebrow Fist from his uncle Qiu Wu, who later recommended him to his own teacher Xia Hanxiong to further practice the Fist and orthopedic medicine, so that Qiu Taisheng made further advances in martial arts and medicine.

仇太生（仇德基供图）
Qiu Taisheng (photo provided by Qiu Deji)

In the early years of the People's Republic of China, Qiu Taisheng and his family moved to Foshan. At the beginning, he worked as a doctor at Li Zibin and Huang Jing's clinic (now on No. 89 Fuxian Road) in the daytime and taught a small number of students martial arts to earn some extra money. In the mid to late 1960s, Qiu had most contact and developed the closest relationship with Liu Shaoliang. Apart from his son Qiu Deji, he passed on White Eyebrow Fist to Lyu Yangzhao, Zhu Caixing, Liao Zhiyi, Li Yinxiang, Feng Yongqiang, Chen San, Barber Ming, Chen Qiu, Liang Yuxi, Xu Wenzheng, Ou Nianzhong and others.

2. Liu Shaoliang, disseminator of White Eyebrow Fist in Foshan

Liu Shaoliang (1905-1977), a native of Shashui, Danzao, the former Nanhai County, lived in Foshan. In his early years when he worked in Yangshan and

Lianxian counties, he learned the superb skills of White Eyebrow Fist from the Taoist Master Zhuyuan (years of birth and death unknown). In 1963, Liu went back to Foshan after his retirement from Guangzhou Machine Tools Factory. He was devoted to promoting and teaching White Eyebrow Fist. Being bosom friends, he and Qiu Taisheng often studied the Fist together.

The 1960s and 1970s witnessed the prosperity of Foshan White Eyebrow Fist. Most of those actively and successfully involved in promoting traditional martial arts were Liu Shaoliang's students.

III. Major organizations of Foshan White Eyebrow Fist

After half a century's dissemination in Foshan, White Eyebrow Fist has had tens of thousands of learners and become an important component of Foshan martial arts. Several major dissemination organizations have been founded successively.

On November 3rd, 1999, White Eyebrow Fist Martial Arts Gymnasium of Foshan Jingwu Sports Association was founded on Xindi Road, Foshan City so that Foshan White Eyebrow Fist has had its own training base. On May 1st, 2003, Foshan Liu Shaoliang Martial Arts Memorial Hall was founded at Lane 10, Shiken No. 1 Village of Foshan. In June 2009, Liu Shaoliang White Eyebrow Fist Gymnasium was founded at Luocun Village, Nanhai, Foshan. In November 2010, White Eyebrow Fist Society of Foshan Martial Arts Association was founded.

In addition, in Nanhai District, a number of martial arts organizations were founded, for example, He Jing Dao Martial Arts Gymnasium of Jinshazhou, Lishui Town in 1999; Martial Arts and Lion Dancing Gymnasium of Beisha, Lishui White Eyebrow in 2004; and White Eyebrow Fist Association of Xiqiao Town in 2006. A lot of people from Foshan have disseminated White Eyebrow Fist to the rest of the world. In 2009, White Eyebrow Fist was listed as a representative project of Foshan Intangible Cultural Heritage, with Huang Xinjian and Huang Guojian as the representative inheritors of the project at the municipal and district levels respectively.

On April 1st, 2004, the Martial Arts and Lion Dancing Gymnasium of Beisha,

白眉拳

White Eyebrow Fist

肯一村十巷。2009年6月，刘少良白眉拳馆在佛山南海罗村开设。2010年11月，佛山市武术协会白眉拳体育总会成立。

此外，在南海区内，1999年成立里水镇金沙洲白眉合劲道武馆，2004年建立南海区里水北沙武术醒狮馆，2006年成立西樵镇白眉拳会。白眉拳由佛山传人传播至世界各地。2009年，白眉拳被列为佛山市非物质文化遗产代表性项目，黄新健、黄国建各为该项目市、区两级代表性传承人。

其中，南海区里水北沙武术醒狮馆于2004年4月1日成立， 前身是“南海区北沙鹤暖岗武术醒狮队”，传承白眉拳和传统南狮。

南海区里水北沙自民国时期已有洪拳、醒狮等传承，近年尤以白眉拳最具特色。佛山市非物质文化遗产白眉拳项目代表性传承人黄新健、黄国建兄弟，其武艺源自张礼泉—曾惠博—陈君侠—陈宗良一脉。

自幼喜爱武术的黄新健、黄国建兄弟，少年时期已在村中学得传统洪拳和初级白眉拳。黄新健在佛山四中读书时也学过白眉拳。后兄弟二人到云浮投于陈宗良门下。随着全民健身活动的普及，黄新健和黄国建又将所学带回家乡南海里水，建立武馆传授之。

（四）佛山白眉拳的主要套路

白眉拳在佛山传播逾半个世纪，因其一直在民间流传，传统套路都是由老师傅口传，其拳谱口诀等记录，根据传入者和所学者的理解，或有变化，不但名称有异，拳谱口诀也各有不同，异

Lishui was founded, its predecessor being Martial Arts and Lion Dancing Team of He'nuangang, Beisha, Nanhai District. It passes on White Eyebrow Fist and the traditional southern school of lion dancing.

During the Republic of China, Hong Quan and lion dancing were already disseminated in Beisha, Lishui of Nanhai District and in recent years White Eyebrow Fist has been most vigorously inherited. Huang Xinjian and Huang Guojian, the two brothers who are representative inheritors of White Eyebrow Fist of Foshan Intangible Cultural Heritage, have acquired their martial arts skills from the line of Zhang Liquan-Zeng Huibo-Chen Junxia-Chen Zongliang. The Huang brothers have loved martial arts since young. In their teens, they already mastered the traditional Hong Quan and preliminary White Eyebrow Fist in the village. Huang Xinjian also learned White Eyebrow Fist when he was a student in Foshan No. 4 Middle School. Later the brothers became students of Chen Zongliang's in Yunfu, Guangdong. With the popularization of fitness activities nationwide, they came back to their hometown with what they had learned and founded the Gymnasium to impart it.

IV. Major routines of White Eyebrow Fist in Foshan

In its dissemination among the Foshan people for more than half a century, White Eyebrow Fist has been passed on orally from the masters to their students, so not only the names of the rouintes, but also the recorded manuals and pithy formulas differ from one to another because of the different understandings of the disseminators and the learners.

The freehand fighting routines passed on from Chen Zongliang to Huang Xinjian and Huang Guojian include Seven-Star Fist, Chain Seven-Star Fist, Cross Fist, Eighteen Hands, Stone Lion Fist, Four-Gate Fist, Three-Gate Fist, Disha Stars Fist, Nine-Step Push, Eighteen Maneuver Bridges, Dragon-Shape and Tiger-Step Maneuver, and *Yin* and *Yang* Maneuver. Major weapon routines include Forest-Exiting Swords (double swords), Plum Blossom Swords (single swords), Hurricane Broadswords, Double-headed Meandering Dragon Clubs, Single-Headed *Yin* and *Yang* Sticks, Rolling Dragon Benches, White Dragon

Spears, Mountain supressing Rakes, Sky-Stirring Halberds, and Rainbow Sabers. In addition, there are major freehand fighting and weapon routines recorded by Qiu Deji and Chen Chengyao respectively.

V. Technical styles of White Eyebrow Fist

Chen Chengyao, who was born in Zhangcha, Foshan in 1944, started learning White Eyebrow Fist from Liu Shaoliang in 1969 and Six-Harmony and Eight-Method Fist from Huang Baixiang later.

Chen was devoted to studying the technical styles of White Eyebrow Fist. Since 1987, he started compiling *Introduction to White Eyebrow Fist* and *Skills and Methods of White Eyebrow Fist*. Chen is one of the few older-generation inheritors of martial arts in Foshan who are good at both arms and arts.

According to Chen, in order to understand the methods, awareness and techniques, one should first understand the commands of "serial heavy hit, straight outward attack and horizontal withdrawal, contradictory transmission, and the combination of offense and defense"; the secrets of "straight upward and downward movement, rapid opening and closing"; and be proficient in the eight methods of "spirit, sense, *qi*, strength, shape, roundness, communication and tranquility". Only with painstaking practices and studies can one enter the high and profound realm. Chen divides the routines of White Eyebrow Fist into four categories—basic, sinking, floating and comprehensive.

彩纷呈。

陈宗良传黄新健、黄国建的拳术套路有七星拳、连环七星拳、十字拳、十八手、石狮拳、四门拳、三门拳、地煞拳、九步推、十八摩桥、龙形虎步摩、两仪神摩等。器械套路有出林刀（双刀）、梅花刀（单刀）、旋风刀（大刀）、游龙棍（双头）、两仪棍（单头）、滚龙凳、白龙枪、镇山耙、混天戟、虹霓剑等。

另有仇德基、陈澄耀的白眉拳谱分别记录的主要拳术套路。

（五）白眉拳的技术风格

1944年出生于佛山张槎的陈澄耀，1969年开始师从刘少良学习白眉拳，其后又随黄佰祥学习六合八法拳。

他致力于研究白眉拳技术风格，从1987年开始整理编写《白眉拳术纵横》和《白眉水拳功与法》等武学心得，是佛山老一辈武术传承者中不可多得的文武兼修的传人。

陈澄耀认为要了解白眉拳的功法、意识和技巧，先要领略“连环重创，直出横收，矛盾传动，攻防合一”十六字令和“直索升沉，开合旋棚”奥秘，精通“神、意、气、劲、形、圆、通、静”八法，潜心研练，才能步入高深境界。他将白眉拳套路根据不同特色分为基础类、沉功类、浮功类、综合性功架类4种。

FOSHAN, CHINA

第五章

佛山武术与传统文化

Chapter 5

Foshan Martial Arts and Traditional Culture

佛山武术与其他传统文化门类关系密切，包括粤剧、醒狮、中医药等。粤剧、醒狮可视为与武术相互包容或衍生，而中医药自武术诞生、传播起即相伴左右。

舞狮
Lion Dancing

Foshan martial arts is closely related to other categories of traditional culture, mainly Cantonese Opera, lion dancing and traditional Chinese medicine (TCM). Martial arts, Cantonese Opera and lion dancing can be considered as mutually inclusive or generative, while TCM has been developing side by side with martial arts since its birth and dissemination.

5.1 Southern Martial Arts and Cantonese Opera

Cantonese Opera, also called Guangdong Opera and Canton Opera, is the largest local opera category in Guangdong Province. It is popular not only in Cantonese-speaking regions of China such as Guangdong, Guangxi, Hong Kong and Macao but also in Shanghai, Tianjin, Taiwan as well as places in Southeast Asia, the Americas, Europe and Oceania where the overseas Chinese of Cantonese descent inhabit.

I. History of Cantonese Opera

In the early Ming .Dynasty, many theatrical troupes from other provinces, commonly known as "Waijiang troupes" (troupes from other provinces), started to perform in Guangdong along with the movement of troops, imperial officials, businessmen and migrants. Vocal tunes of Yiyang, Kunshan, Bangzi and Erhuang gradually spread to different parts of Guangdong, making local opera activities thrive. After fixed stages were built in the Pearl River Delta, opera performances had become more active and professional, attracting more and more local people to be performers.

In the Qing Dynasty, early theatrical troupes in Foshan were categorized into Waijiang troupes and local troupes. Local troupes were distinctive in art, especially in acrobatic fighting and stunts, as a result of the solid foundation of traditional martial arts in Foshan. The following are three major martial arts practicing sites and their related personnel.

1. Qionghua Guild Hall in Foshan, the earliest guild hall of Cantonese Opera

Qionghua Guild Hall in Foshan is the earliest association for the artists of local

第一节 南派武术与粤剧

粤剧是广东省最大的地方戏曲剧种，又称广东大戏、广府戏等，流行于两广、港澳等粤语地区和上海、天津、台湾等地，以及东南亚、美洲、欧洲、大洋洲等粤籍华侨、华人聚居的地方。

（一）粤剧历史渊源

明初，由于军旅、游宦、经商、移民等原因，众多俗称“外江班”的外省戏班开始入粤演出。弋阳、昆山、梆子、二黄等声腔逐渐流入广东各地，使广东的戏剧活动蓬勃兴起，珠江三角洲开始建有固定的戏台，演出活动日益活跃和专业化，广东本地人也加入了演出的行列。

清代佛山早期的戏班，有外江班与本地班之分。佛山传统武术根基深厚，本地班表演艺术特色鲜明，在武打和特技方面尤为卓绝，形成如下3个主要习武场所与相关人员：

1. 粤剧最早的会馆——琼花会馆

佛山琼花会馆是本地班艺人最早的行会组织。当年在本地戏班中，武生唱主角，具有较高地位。

2. 江湖漂泊的红船子弟

“红船”为本地班的代名词，伶人也称为红船子弟。在外谋生的红船子弟，为求平安需要有武艺防身，为博观众喝彩也需武艺超群，因此武角在班中的地位十分重要，练功也是他们每天必做的事情。

红船上练功的木人桩

A wooden dummy used for practicing Martial Arts on a red boat

3. 銮舆堂与木人桩

广州八和会馆的銮舆堂至今仍保存着武打演员用于训练的木人桩和桩谱。这套木人桩20世纪80年代由出身于武术世家的著名武打演员梁金峰捐献。梁金峰还连同其大哥梁天斗、弟弟梁少棠整理了108式桩谱，并自己出资将木人桩的规范动作和要领拍摄下来，制成录像带，成为当今粤剧南派武功的教学示范。

（二）粤剧武打名伶

清代雍正年间，有北京名伶张五，演唱皆妙。他宗少林派武功，为反清义士，为避清廷追杀，隐身佛山大基尾红船班中，秘密

troupes. In those days, male martial actors played the leading roles in local troupes and enjoyed high status.

2. Artists of the red boats that drifted around

The red boats that were used to transport troupes around the Pearl River Delta were synonymous of local Cantonese Opera troupes. Artists of such troupes were also called red boat artists. For them, martial arts were necessary not only for protecting themselves but also for entertaining the audience. Given the importance of martial roles, actors had to practice martial arts every day.

3. Luanyu Hall and the wooden dummy

The wooden dummy and pictures of martial skills used by the martial actors for practice are still well preserved in Luanyu Hall of Guangzhou Bahe Guild. The wooden dummy was donated in the 1980s by Liang Jinfeng, a renowned martial actor who came from a martial arts family. Liang Jinfeng, together with his elder brother Liang Tiandou and younger brother Liang Shaotang, sorted out pictures of 108 stake skills, filmed standard movements and main points of practicing with the wooden dummy at his own expense and made them into a video clip which has become a teaching demonstration of southern martial arts in Cantonese Opera.

II. Renowned martial arts actors in Cantonese Opera

During the Yongzheng period of the Qing Dynasty, a famous artist named Zhang Wu in Beijing was known for his wonderful singing and acting skills. He practiced Shaolin martial arts and was an anti-Qing fighter. In order to avoid persecution by the Qing Dynasty, he hid himself in a red boat in Dajiwei, Foshan and secretly taught other artists martial arts. Martial actor Huang Huabao and minor martial actor Liang Erdi were on the boat too, both of whom were of great attainments in martial arts. Liang Zan of Foshan learned martial arts from them and passed on Yongchun Quan to later generations.

In support of the Taiping Rebellion and with Jingtang Ancient Temple as the governor's office, Li Wenmao, a red boat artist of Fenghuangyi Troupe in Foshan led Cantonese Opera artists to launch an uprising together with Chen Kai, the leader of the Heaven and Earth Society.

III.Characteristics of Southern martial arts in Cantonese Opera

In the early days, local troupes of Cantonese Opera mainly performed plays with a lot of action scenes. Artists consciously absorbed the moves and routines of local martial arts styles such as Hong Quan, Yongchun Quan and Cai Li Fo Quan, so a lot of moves maintained distinctive characteristics of southern martial arts. Cantonese Opera artists should master the "four skills" of singing, acting, speech delivery and martial skills and the "five methods" associated with the hands, eyes, body, rules, and steps. Other distinctive basic skills include Pulling the Mountains (basic movements of arms and hands), *Cheshen* (stretching two hands to the left and right with one palm up and the other down and then twirling), Small Jump (stamping before walking), *Tijia* (kicking up the hem of the costume), *Taqixing* (taking seven steps in the shape of the Big Dipper), etc. In addition, there are other special moves and stunts, such as the Eighteen Lohans. It is a form of performance with great expressiveness which imitates the posture of eighteen Lohans and integrates different styles of Southern martial arts.

传统例戏《六国大封相》中的"打跟斗"

A somersault scene in the traditional ceremonial play *A Prime Minister Who Carries Seals of Six Hostile Kingdoms*

Southern martial arts in Cantonese Opera attach great importance to practical use, so what artists perform are usually real fighting skills learned from folk martial arts masters. For example, Liang Yintang, a martial actor hailed as the *Tanhua* (ranking the third among his kind) in Cantonese Opera, successively

传授技艺。红船中又有武生黄华宝、小武梁二娣，都是身怀绝世武功的人物。佛山梁赞师从黄、梁二师，传咏春拳于后世。

佛山凤凰仪班的红船弟子李文茂响应太平天国运动，以佛山经堂古寺为都督府，率领粤剧艺人会同天地会首领陈开发动起义。

（三）粤剧艺术中的南派武功特征

粤剧早期本地班表演武戏居多。粤剧舞台的武打动作都有意识地吸收了地方武术洪拳、咏春拳、蔡李佛拳等拳种的招式、套路，故舞台上许多武打动作都留有鲜明的南派武术烙印。粤剧演员的唱、做、念、打“四功”和手、眼、身、法、步“五法”均为基本功，较有特色的粤剧表演基本功有拉山、车身、小跳、踢甲、踏七星等。除此之外，还有许多特殊的功架身段和特技。十八罗汉架是粤剧表演程式，它模仿寺庙十八罗汉的姿态，融汇了南派武功艺术，表现力丰富。

粤剧南派武功注重实用，表演的多是真功夫，武打演员一般都曾跟随民间武术师傅习艺。有粤剧

粤剧
Cantonese Opera

“武探花”之誉的著名演员梁荫棠，曾先后拜师著名武术家陈斗、程君侠习武。

传统武术在粤剧中的运用，见证了其对粤剧艺术的重要影响。传统武术是粤剧艺术宝库中极其珍贵的一部分。

（四）抢救粤剧南派武功现代进行时

20世纪30年代是粤剧南派武功的变动时期。在这一时期，粤剧形成了一股崇尚北派武打之风，甚至以北派武功代替了南派武功，南派武功特色逐渐淡化。

近年来，在一些有识之士的倡议下，粤剧南派武功逐渐受到关注。佛山粤剧传习所整合粤剧文化资源，打造全国知名的戏剧文化聚集地，深入挖掘粤剧南派武功传统剧目。

learned martial arts from Chen Dou and Cheng Junxia, two great martial arts masters.

The application of traditional martial arts in Cantonese Opera has witnessed the significant impact of the former on the latter. Traditional martial arts are an extremely precious part of the treasure house of Cantonese Opera.

IV. Current efforts to rescue southern martial arts in Cantonese Opera

In the 1930s, southern martial arts in Cantonese Opera experienced some changes. At that time, actors preferred performing northern martial arts and even replaced the southern martial arts skills with the northern ones. As a result, the feature of southern acrobatic fighting movements in Cantonese Opera gradually faded.

In recent years, due to the advocacy of people with vision, southern martial arts have gained increasing public attention. Foshan Cantonese Opera Promotion and Study Institute, by integrating cultural resources of Cantonese Opera, has developed into a nationally renowned place for drama culture and explored traditional Cantonese Opera repertoire with Southern martial arts.

万福台
Wanfu (Ten-Thousand Blessings) Stage

5.2 Foshan Martial Arts and Traditional Lion Dancing

I. The origin of Foshan lion dancing

Chinese lion dancing has two main forms, the northern lion dancing, which came into being the earliest, and the southern lion dancing. The southern lion dancing, represented by Cantonese one, originated in Foshan and is popular in the coastal areas of South China, Southeast Asia and other countries and regions. It is one of the most influential folk lion dances. There is no clear record of the origin of the southern lion dancing, and it is said that it evolved from the northern one. But the most widely circulated story is about the mythical monster Nian.

Legend has it that long long ago, in Dasha Village, Zhangcha, Foshan, the drooping ears of rice were promising a bumper harvest in autumn. Unexpectedly, at this time there appeared a one-horned monster, ruining crops in the middle of the night. The villagers tried to capture it, but the monster rushed left and right and made the deafening sounds. They could do nothing to fend it off. Then, an experienced elder proposed, "The lion is the king of the beasts. If we want to subdue the fierce monster, we must rely on the lion." The villagers all agreed. But where could they find a lion? Someone came up with a way—make a lion's head with bamboo sticks, draw the facial features and the fur of the lion on a piece of cloth, and choose a man with a strong body and quick action to disguise as a live lion to scare the monster off while at the same time, drums and gongs would be beaten boisterously, and all the villagers yell with one voice, to cheer for

第二节 佛山武术与传统醒狮

（一）佛山醒狮的来源

醒狮，又称舞狮或狮子舞。中国舞狮，以北方狮子舞起源最早。南派舞狮，以广东醒狮为代表，起源于佛山，流行于我国南部沿海地区及东南亚等地区，是最具影响力的民间狮子舞之一。关于南派舞狮的起源没有明确记载，有说是由北派舞狮演变而来，流传最广的是关于年兽的故事。

相传，很久以前，佛山张槎大沙村内稻穗飘香，秋收在望。谁曾想这时却出现了一只独角怪兽，深夜出没糟蹋庄稼，村民围追堵截，怪兽左冲右突，还发出震耳欲聋的怪叫，村民无计可施。这时，一位有阅历的长者提出：狮子乃百兽之王，要降服那凶残的怪兽，非狮子莫属。众人赞同，但狮子何来呢？有人想出办法：用竹篾编扎成狮子头模样的头套，在布上画出狮子的五官和身上的毛，并选择身体壮实、行动敏捷、精灵的男子，把“狮子头”套在头上，装扮成活狮子的模样，到时敲响锣鼓，全村男女老少齐声呐喊，为“狮子”助威。这个办法果然奏效，那只独角怪兽竟被吓住，再也不敢来摧残农作物。自此，舞狮逐渐普及，成为独特的民间风俗。

舞狮
Lion Dancing

（二）佛山醒狮的武术特征

相传，将武术融入南派舞狮与反清复明组织天地会有关。当时清廷为防止汉人作乱，下令禁止汉人习武和集会。于是，练武的人只能关门“修炼”而不敢公开。戏班中人由于有戏剧的基础，很快就想到了办法，就是利用舞狮子来练武，扎狮头时大量采用拟人化的手法，将戏剧人物脸谱应用到狮头纹样装饰中。从此，南派舞狮的狮剧开始形成，在舞狮技术上除了原有的大头狮的舞法外，还融入了武术的步法、身法、手法、腿法，再结合粤剧功架，使得狮剧的表演更有观赏性、更威猛，有效地掩饰了练武的性质。

佛山舞狮写意，善用拟人手法结合粤剧做功和南派武术，以身体语言讲故事的形式进行演绎。

佛山民间武术的兴起，推

the "lion". This method worked. The monster was scared away and never dared to damage the crops again. From then on, lion dancing has gradually become a popular and unique folk custom.

II. The martial arts characteristics of Foshan lion dancing

The integration of martial arts into the southern lion dancing was said to be related to the Heaven and Earth Society, whose mission was to "oppose the Qing and restore the Ming". At the time, in order to prevent the Han Chinese from rioting, the Qing court prohibited them from practicing martial arts and from gathering. Therefore, those who practiced martial arts could only do so secretly. People in the theatrical troupes had much drama experience, so they soon came up with an idea, i.e. to practice martial arts in disguise of lion dancing. The lion's head was made in an anthropomorphic way, decorated with the facial expressions of drama characters. Since then, the southern lion dancing came into being. In terms of lion dancing techniques, in addition to the original Big Head Lion dance, it also incorporates martial arts techniques of the feet, body, hands and legs, as well as Cantonese Opera postures and movements, making lion drama performances more entertaining and more forceful, thus effectively covering up the intention to practice martial arts.

Foshan lion dancing makes good use of anthropomorphic techniques and combines with Cantonese Opera and southern martial arts to tell stories in the form of body language.

The rise of Foshan folk martial arts has promoted the development of mass lion dancing activities, and many martial arts organizations have established lion dancing clubs. According to Yu Wanshao, a Foshan folklorist, from the late Qing Dynasty to the Republic of China, except Liang Zan Martial Arts Gymnasium of Yongchun Quan, almost all the halls and societies belonging to other schools of Foshan martial arts, such as Cai Li Fo, Yongchun, and Shaolin, had set up lion dancing clubs, which contained their respective martial arts skills.

Foshan lion dancing usually uses an anthropomorphic way to tell the story. In order to identify the relationship between Hongmen's different halls, it is specified that right before the lion dancing, the dancers would perform some martial arts movements with certain gestures (hand movements and sign language), which can reflect the characteristics of each martial arts type. This is now the ritual stake performance of Foshan lion dancing. Insiders can know instantly which club the dancers belong to.

III. The unique Foshan "Three Sages Lions"

The "Three Sages Lions" is a traditional lion dance based on the stories of Liu Bei, Guan Yu, and Zhang Fei during the Three Kingdoms period, and combined with the make-up of different characters, stage performances of Cantonese Opera and southern martial arts. The Three Sages Lions refer to the lions of Liu

广东醒狮省级传承人何狄强演示狮艺（何狄强供图）
He Diqiang, a provincial inheritor of Guangdong Lion Dancing, demonstrating the art of lion dancing (photo provided by He himself)

动了群众舞狮活动的发展，众多武馆组织都建立了狮会。据佛山民俗学者余婉韶统计，清末至民国时期，佛山蔡李佛拳、咏春拳、少林等各派武馆属下的堂、社，除咏春派的梁赞武馆没有设立狮会外，几乎都设立了狮会。各派功夫蕴含其中。

由于佛山舞狮在演绎上更多的是用拟人手法讲述故事，为了识别洪门各山堂的关系，还特定在舞狮前，按照各派拳种的特点，将手势（手印、手语）融入武术中。舞狮人先表演几下武术功夫，再进行舞狮，这就是现在佛山舞狮的开桩礼。内行观看，便知是哪个门派的舞狮了。

（三）独具特色的佛山“三圣狮”

“三圣狮”是以三国时期刘备、关羽、张飞的人物故事为题材，糅合粤剧艺术中的戏剧脸谱、舞台功架，以及南派武术而演绎的传统狮艺。“三圣狮”指“刘备狮”“关羽狮”和“张飞狮”，用拟人化方式表现醒狮艺术。传统“三圣狮”的鼓乐，文场用三声（星）鼓，武场用七声（星）鼓，文武场用三七声（星）鼓。舞狮的桥马完全采用南派武术之四平马、子午马、丁字马、座盘马和吊蹄马等，步法有麒麟步、碎步、马步、弓步、虚步、行步、探步、插步、提步、摆步、丁步、趟步、扑步、跳步等。

在各派武术的历史发展和传习过程中，各武馆结合自身所练武术的特点、自家功夫的鼓点，加上狮舞的编排，形成了当今异彩纷呈的“三圣狮”艺术特色。

（四）佛山醒狮的身体语言

过去学舞狮，必先学功夫，武功扎实者，狮子舞起来也特别威风凛凛，雄壮有力。佛山醒狮是民众喜闻乐见的一种既可驱魔镇邪又有娱乐性的活动，具有独特的身体语言，行内的人一看就能分辨出各山堂及其传递的信息和内容。

相传民间秘密组织天地会利用舞狮活动作为掩饰，将三圣狮舞作为传递信息的方法，推动反清力量的组织和扩展。

天地会以“反清复明”为宗旨，舞狮中加入了狮子采青的环节——“采青”谐音“踩清”，即把清廷踩在脚下，后演绎出当今的诸多表现程式。又因“狮”与“输”谐音，民间忌讳“输”，故又把舞狮称为“舞胜头”，传统醒狮的身体语言因而有了更多的表达方式和信息传递方法。

（五）舞者与武者

顺德咏春拳传人陈锦良言：“传统的舞狮和武术是不分家的，舞狮者也是武术者。”

随着佛山的武术和醒狮活动蓬勃发展，大批拳师和著名的舞狮教头涌现。目前，佛山国家级非物质文化遗产项目广东醒狮的代表性传承人，除醒狮技艺各有师承外，其武术传承也自有渊源。

Bei, Guan Yu, and Zhang Fei. The traditional drumming of the Three Sages Lions uses different beats for civil and martial scenes. The lion dance adopts the typical stances and steps of southern martial arts.

In the process of the development and inheritance of various styles of martial arts, the martial arts clubs, by combining traditional lion dancing with the characteristics of their own martial arts and drumming, have formed the colorful artistic feature of "Three Sages Lions".

IV. Body language of Foshan lion dancing

In the past, one must learn martial arts first before learning lion dancing. For those who have solid martial arts skills, their lion dancing is also particularly majestic and powerful. Foshan lion dancing is a popular activity that can exorcize the evils and entertain people. With its unique body language, people in the industry can distinguish the various martial arts schools or clubs, and the information the dance conveys at a glance.

It is said that the Heaven and Earth Society, the underground organization, used the Three Sages Lions as a cover-up to convey information as they promoted the organization and expansion of anti-Qing forces.

The Heaven and Earth Society, with "opposing the Qing and restoring the Ming" as its tenet, added the activity called *Caiqing* (collecting the greens) to the lion dance. Caiqing in Chinese is homophnic with trampling on the Qing Dynasty. It has evolved into many different presentations nowadays. In addition, because the Chinese characters of "lion" and "lose" have similar pronunciations, people also call lion dancing "dancing the winning head" to avoid the taboo of "lose". Therefore, the body language of traditional lion dancing conveys a lot of expressions and information.

V. Lion dancers and martial arts practitioners

Chen Jinliang, the inheritor of Shunde Yongchun Quan, once said, "Traditional lion dancing and martial arts are inseparable; a lion dancer is also a martial arts practitioner."

With the flourishing of martial arts and lion dancing activities in Foshan, there have emerged a large number of martial arts masters and famous lion dancers. At present, the representative inheritors of Guangdong Lion Dancing—one of the National Intangible Cultural Heritage items in Foshan, have their own origins in martial arts as well as their lion dance skills.

VI. The artistic style of Foshan lion dancing

Foshan lion dancing, with a history of hundreds of years, has formed its distinctive style in the process of inheritance. Martial arts and art are ingeniously combined to create perfect and vivid images. The lion dancing skills are closely related to martial arts as they have absorbed the stances, footwork and other postures and movements of various martial arts clubs and styles to express the eight moods and states of lions, including happiness, anger, drunkenness, joy, movement, stillness, shock, and suspicion. Thanks to the postures and movements of martial arts, lion dancing is more lively and expressive.

Foshan lions have a strong ethnic style in appearance. They have rich colors and unique decorations, with the facial make-up of characters in opera applied to the lion heads to indicate different personalities of different lions.

佛山醒狮赴京参加中华人民共和国成立五十周年表演（夏志成供图）
Foshan Lion Dancing Team participating in the performance of the 50th Anniversary of the Founding of the People's Republic of China in Beijing (photo provided by Xia Zhicheng)

（六）佛山醒狮的艺术风格

佛山醒狮已有数百年历史，在传承的过程中形成鲜明的风格。武术和艺术巧妙结合，塑造出生动完美的形象。醒狮的舞法，与武术密不可分，它吸纳了各武馆、各流派的步型、步法、功架，并将其糅合到舞狮中去，表现狮子喜、怒、醉、乐、动、静、惊、疑八态。武术的功架技巧，使醒狮更生动传神。

佛山醒狮在造型上彰显了浓郁的民族风情，色彩丰富，纹饰独特，用拟人化的手法，将舞台上的人物角色脸谱运用于狮头设色上，显示不同狮子的不同个性。

第三节　佛山武术与中医药

在我国文化发展史中，传统武术与传统中医有着共同理论渊源。佛山武术在世代沿袭的基础上发展迅速，传播广泛。手工劳作及武术兴盛等诸多因素，使筋伤骨断之事时有出现，为中医伤科正骨提供了丰富的临床实践机会，为中成药研制及应用提供了广阔的市场。

不少能医者，本身就是习武者，如咏春拳宗师梁赞，开设荣生堂医馆；洪拳一代宗师黄飞鸿，开设宝芝林医馆；阮奇山家族有阮时和堂；还有梁财信医馆、陈华顺医馆、梁细苏医馆、李广海医馆等。他们医武同研，以精确的理伤手法及有效的伤科药剂著称于世，留下了不朽的传奇。

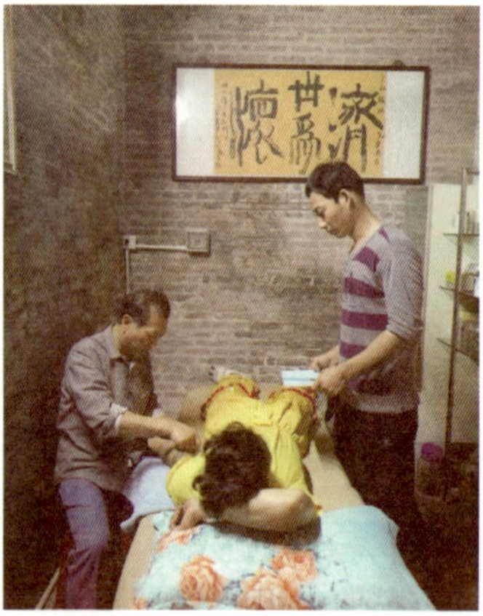

林世荣之孙林镇成用家传药酒与手法为患者治病

Lam Chun Sing (Lin Shirong's grandson) treating a patient with family medicinal liquor and techniques

洪拳一代宗师黄飞鸿，不但武艺高强，狮艺精湛，中医

5.3 Foshan Martial Arts and Traditional Chinese Medicine (TCM)

In the history of China's cultural development, traditional martial arts and TCM share the same theoretical foundations. On the basis of centuries' inheritance, Foshan martial arts have developed rapidly and spread widely. Because of manual labor and the popularity of martial arts, it was common to have injured tendons or broken bones, which had offered abundant clinical opportunities for orthopedics of TCM as well as vast markets for the development and application of TCM pharmaceutics.

Many doctors were martial arts practitioners, such as Rong Sheng Tang Medical Hall by Yongchun Master Liang Zan, "Baozhilin" Medical Hall by Hong Quan Master Huang Feihong, and Ruan Shi He Tang Medical Hall by the Ruan Qishan family. There were also Liang Caixin Medical Hall, Chen Huashun Medical Hall, Liang Xisu Medical Hall, and Li Guanghai Medical Hall. The martial arts masters studied both martial arts and medicine so that they were well known for their precise treatments and effective traumatologic medicines.

Hong Quan Master Huang Feihong not only had superb martial arts and lion dancing skills, but also extraordinary TCM skills. When he was teaching martial arts in the army, it was inevitable that some practitioners got injured. Because of his family medical skills and unique prescriptions, he treated them effectively and accumulated clinical experience. He made a name for himself by curing the arm injury of Zhang Zhidong, the then Governor of Guangdong and Guangxi.

Foshan is the "Hometown of Patent Medicine in Lingnan". In the past, the patent TCM industry was developed, with martial arts-related orthopedic patent TCMs as its most outstanding specialty drugs. In addition to the factory-

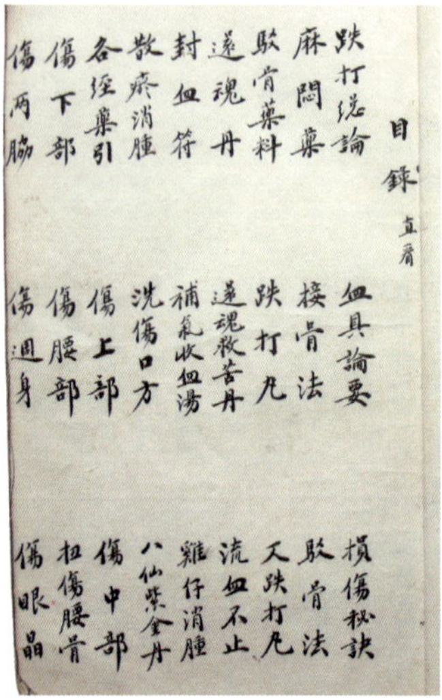
目錄

跌打總論 麻悶藥 駁骨藥料 還魂丹 封血符 散瘀消腫 各經藥引 傷下部 傷兩脇

血具論要 接骨法 跌打丸 還魂救苦丹 補氣收血湯 洗傷口方 傷上部 傷腰部 傷週身

損傷秘訣 駁骨法 又跌打丸 流血不止 雜仔消腫 八仙紫金丹 傷中部 扭傷腰骨 傷眼晶

南家拳门人传抄的医方目录
A table of contents of medical prescriptions copied among disciples of the Nan Jia Quan

produced orthopedic medicines, various methods and prescriptions to treat bruises and injuries by different schools of Foshan martial arts have been circulating among the people. As the proverb goes, "Before learning martial arts, one should learn orthopedics first". Along with martial arts, folk medicines and prescriptions have been inherited in the respective schools.

It is believed that the legendary martial arts scriptures include not only freehand fighting and weapon routines or precepts, but also orthopedic prescriptions and medication methods. The many traditional medical manuscripts of the various schools of Foshan martial arts provide precious treasures for us to further study the internal relationship between martial arts and TCM.

药技术更是高超。他在军中传授武术，习练者损伤在所难免，作为武术教官，他有家传医术和独到的医方，当然能一显身手，同时也积累了临床经验。他治好了两广总督张之洞的臂伤，名噪一时。

佛山是“岭南成药之乡”，早期中成药制药业发达，与武术相关的跌打类成药最具特色。除了设厂生产的跌打成药外，佛山各派拳种跌打治伤方法和用药秘方一直在民间流传。谚语有云：“未学武术，先学跌打。”在武术传承的同时，民间医术和药方也在各自门内传承至今。

传说中的武林秘籍，相信除了师傅传授的拳械套路或心法外，跌打医方和用药方法也是其中的一部分。佛山武术各门派中的许多传统医药稿本，是我们进一步研究武术和中医药之间内在关系的宝贵财富。

FOSHAN, CHINA

结语

Conclusion

武术不仅是一种文化，一种传统技艺，一种现代强身健体的手段，更关系民族的强健体魄和国家的强盛复兴。佛山武术历史悠久、泽被当世。武术文化已然成为佛山一张闪亮的城市名片。伴随历史长河的流淌，在新时代文化复兴的洪流中，佛山武术文化必会更加熠熠生辉。

Martial arts are not only a culture, a traditional technique and a modern means to keep fit, but also closely related to the health and strength of the nation and the prosperity and revival of the whole country. Foshan martial arts have had a long history and benefited the contemporary society, so martial arts culture has become an outstanding city card. With the progress of history, they will continue to shine in the torrents of cultural renaissance in the new era.

1 A Long History

The time-honored Chinese martial arts have come into being and developed side by side with the Chinese civilization and Foshan martial arts are an integral part of the rich and colorful Chinese martial arts culture.

The Han Dynasty swords and other weapons unearthed from tombs in Xuwen and Shaoguan of Guangdong Province show that martial arts were already popular at that time. The bronze swords of the Western Han Dynasty unearthed from Hougang, Lanshi of Foshan can serve as physical evidences of martial arts development in Lingnan.

In the second year of the Zhen'guan period (628) of the Tang Dynasty, Foshan developed into a town from the original 15 natural villages and township economy started to take shape. In the Tang and Song dynasties, Chinese martial arts developed rapidly and gradually matured.

In the Song Dynasty, Zhaxia, Foshan where there were important sea passages was stationed by officials from the city shipping department and was equipped with cannons at the waterfront. The Song Dynasty, following the system of the Later Zhou during the Five Dynasties and Ten Kingdoms period, established the village militia, so folk martial arts and various weapons came into being one after another. In order to fight against foreign invasion and pirates, the villagers worked on their own advantages and practiced martial arts together for self-defense.

In the Ming and Qing dynasties, with the prosperity of Guangdong's foreign trade, Foshan, with its superb geographical location, accelerated its economic development. Handicrafts such as foundry, ceramics, textiles, and patent TCM as well as the market economy developed on a large scale. Foshan became known

第一节　历史悠久

中国武术，源远流长，武术的萌生和发展，伴随着华夏文明的发展，佛山武术是中华瑰丽多姿武术文化中的一个有机组成部分。

从广东徐闻、韶关等墓葬出土的汉代刀、剑兵器可知，当时习武从戎渐成风尚；佛山澜石后岗西汉墓葬出土的青铜剑，或可作为岭南武术发展的实物例证。

唐贞观二年（628），佛山地区的15个自然小村落已呈聚拢趋势，城镇经济开始形成。唐宋时期，中国武术迅速发展，并逐步走向成熟。

宋代佛山栅下海舶要冲有市舶司提举官员驻守，设有临海炮台，且宋朝承袭后周遗制，设置乡兵，民间拳术和多种器械使用开始涌现。为抗击外侵和海盗滋扰，乡村百姓各占形势，结社练武，屯聚自保。

明清时期，随着广东对外贸易繁荣，具有地理优势的佛山经济发展日益加快，铸造、制陶、纺织、中成药等手工业和市场经济形成规模。户口之繁、物产之富、文物之盛，使佛山闻名于中外，跻身天下“四大名镇”之冠。

成熟的冶铁铸造技术使佛山成为我国武器生产的重要基地之

一，各种制式的铁炮、大铳、流弹等产品，为军事对抗和势力抗争提供了物质基础。从明代正统年间黄萧养起事和由地方耆老所组织的军事防御可以看到，武器的制造在当时佛山已成行业，而使用这些武器的人，已经过长期的训练并有技术的支撑，这也反映了当时佛山已经拥有使用这些兵器的人才。

黄萧养起事加快了佛山内部社区治理制度形成的步伐，民间自卫性质的忠义营逐步向团练发展，形成规模，使武术在佛山有了较好的根基，同时促使了佛山市镇与周围农村的分离，城镇化建设步伐不断加快。

工商业、手工业经济迅速发展，使各方人才大量涌入佛山，外来拳种在佛山落地后，发展空间广阔，逐步与本地原有武术相结合，形成自己的风格；经济的发展也使武术、舞狮等在各种神诞庙会等民俗活动中扮演了重要的角色。

明清时期武科制度推行，为广东武术人才储备提供了先决条件，这个时期广东5名武状元中佛山就占其二。清康熙年间，佛山、南海区域的武进士和武举人数量激增，民间习武已成风尚。武术在这一片土地上具有广阔的应用空间，南派武术得以孕育并较好地发展。

清代中期，尤其是鸦片战争后，国势日衰，国民积弱暴露无遗，为了内固疆国，外抗强寇，练习武技蔚然成风。

佛山粤剧艺人李文茂与广东天地会首领陈开策动的起义，率领粤剧艺人及大批民众加入抗清运动洪流，这股世人称为“洪兵”的力量，在清廷的高压政策下，随着转战两广地区而流播各地。部分

at home and abroad because of its large population, rich products and prosperous cultural relics. It topped the "Four Famous Towns" in China.

Mature smelting and foundry techniques made Foshan one of the most important bases of weapon production in China. Iron cannons, blunderbusses, stray bullets and other weapons produced in Foshan provided material bases for military confrontations and power struggles. As can be seen from the Huang Xiaoyang Rebellion and the military defense organized by village elders, weapon production had developed into an industry in Foshan and those people using these weapons had received long-term training and technical support. All these have reflected that back then, there were already talent who could use these weapons.

Huang Xiaoyang Rebellion accelerated the formation of the internal governance system of business zones in Foshan. The loyalty and righteousness camps for self-defense developed into large-scale training groups, laying a solid foundation for martial arts in Foshan. It also boosted the separation of towns from the surrounding villages, thus accelerating Foshan's urbanization.

The rapid development of industry, commerce and handicrafts led to the large influx of population into Foshan. After martial arts types from other places took root in Foshan, they had large space for development and gradually formed their own styles by integrating with the local varieties. The economic development also enabled martial arts and lion dancing to play important roles in various folk activities such as deity birthday celebrations and temple fairs.

The implementation of imperial martial examinations during the Ming and Qing dynasties provided prerequisites for the increasing martial arts talent in Guangdong. During this time, two of the five martial champions from Guangdong in the imperial examinations were from Foshan. During the Kangxi period of the Qing Dynasty, the numbers of metropolitan and provincial graduates from martial examinations from Foshan and Nanhai surged, where martial arts had become a fashion and had vast potential for application. As a result, southern martial arts were bred and well developed.

In the mid Qing Dynasty, especially after the Opium War in 1840, China's national power went from bad to worse, fully exposing the weaknesses of the country and the people. In order to consolidate the borders and fight against foreign invaders, martial arts were widely practiced.

Li Wenmao, a Foshan Cantonese artist, and Chen Kai, head of the Guangdong Heaven and Earth Society, led the Cantonese Opera actors and actresses and the general public to join in the rebellion against the Qing Dynasty, and they were called the "Hong Army". Under the high pressure of the Qing court, this force was compelled to fight in Guangdong, Guangxi and other places, thus spreading their martial arts skills. Some of them fled abroad and spread martial arts to countries such as Singapore and Malaysia.

Against such historical backdrops, folk martial arts have kept developing and formed an independent martial arts system represented by Hong Quan, Liu Jia Quan, Cai Jia Quan, Li Jia Quan and Mo Jia Quan. The contents and formulas of lion dancing have also been enriched.

The rapid development of industry, commence and handicrafts in Foshan attracted people from various places. In order to meet the needs of the working people and the martial arts learners, orthopedic techniques and pharmaceutics were fully utilized and developed in Foshan.

In the Qing Dynasty, among the five major martial arts types in Guangdong, Hong Quan was the most widely spread and the most renowned. The martial arts stories of Tie Qiao San, Lin Fucheng, Lu Yacai, Huang Qiying, Huang Feihong and Lin Shirong became materials repetitively used by novelists in the late Qing Dynasty and the early Republic of China. With the promotion of cultural products, Huang Feihong's chivalrous spirit of righteousness and justice, and of beating the strong and helping the weak has become an exemplar of Chinese martial arts spirit.

Yongchun Quan was introduced into Foshan mainly through local opera troupes which drifted around. On the one hand, these Shaolin martial skills were spread to various places by the Red Boat artists; on the other hand, they were spread and developed by the locals, who had formed huge groups to pass on the martial arts from one generation to the next, such as Liang Zan and his followers Chen Huashun, Chen Rumian, Zhao Jiu, Li Yechi, Ye Wen (Yip Man) and Peng Nan; Ruan Jiyun and his followers Yao Cai, Yao Qi, Lin Ruiwen and Lin Ruibo; Feng

身怀绝技的艺人辗转逃生，还将武术的种子传播至新加坡、马来西亚等异国他乡。

在这一历史背景下，武术在广东民间不断丰富和发展，出现了以洪拳、刘家拳、蔡家拳、李家拳、莫家拳这五大名拳为代表的独立拳种体系，舞狮的内容程式也增添了丰富的内涵。

佛山工商业、手工业的迅速发展汇聚了五方之众，应生活劳作和武术研习人群等的大量需求，跌打伤科正骨技艺及制药技艺在佛山得到充分的利用和发展。

清代广东五大名拳中，洪拳在佛山传播最广、名声最盛。铁桥三、林福成、陆亚采、黄麒英、黄飞鸿、林世荣等洪拳名家在佛山武林的事迹，成为晚清和民国时期小说家反复运用的题材。随着文化产品的有力推动，黄飞鸿刚直正义、锄强扶弱的侠义气概，更成为中华武术精神的典范。

咏春拳传入佛山主要通过清代漂泊的本地戏班，这些少林嫡传武技一方面随着红船子弟流播各地，另一方面由本地人学成后扎根本土繁衍传播。佛山梁赞及其之后的陈华顺、陈汝棉、招就、黎叶篪、叶问、彭南等，阮济云及其之后的姚才、姚祺、林瑞文、林瑞波等，冯少青及其之后的阮奇山、张保、岑能、邓算等，还有咏春拳的各派支脉及其传人，构成了佛山功夫数代传承的庞大群体。

在晚清社会变革的动荡中，蔡李佛拳传入佛山。清咸丰元年（1851），张炎在佛山创立鸿胜馆，扎根于社会最基层，与劳苦大众同呼吸、共命运。在多次社会变革中，鸿胜馆的主要骨干走在革新的最前列，在反封建、反压迫等的工人运动和农民运动斗争中发挥了重要作用。随后，该组织也受到当政者的压制，在1927年后销声匿迹长达10年，众多拳师远赴香港和海外设馆授徒。

在20世纪30年代后期，鸿胜馆组织以体育会形式再生，在当时的政治环境下虽然备受制约，但仍然在狭缝中抗争求存，延续活力，其弟子多次击败外国拳师，扬威海内外。

清末民初出现在佛山的南家拳，以梁细苏为宗师。他个性低调，隐而不彰，使武术界只闻其名，不明其拳种所属，根源扑朔迷离。该拳种内涵丰富，在佛山传承百年，应为中原武术南来发展的又一例证。

民国初期，广东曾举办国术竞赛选拔人才以服务于当时的军界，民间拳师如洪拳的林世荣、白眉拳的张礼泉、龙形拳的林耀桂等均在李福林军队中当过武术教头。

周家拳的周龙也是当中一员，他融合所学洪拳、蔡家拳及少林功夫，开宗立派，与其弟共五人以“周家五虎”之名享誉武林。周彪、周海兄弟在广东精武会成立之时曾与黄飞鸿、林世荣等同台献艺。该拳种在两广地区传播甚广，佛山顺德、南海均有支脉传承。20世纪30年代传播至海外，周馆遍布世界各地。

随着西方近代体育的传入，传统武术中之有识之士也力求在时代变革中求新和发展。精武体育会的建立，打破了民间原来各种练武组织的组织与活动方式及宗法或宗教色彩，采用了现代体育组织和学校这一全新的武术传播方式，推动了武术现代化与国际化的进程，开辟和彰显了武术的诸多价值功能。精武体育会成为促进武术现代化转型发展的先锋与楷模。

Shaoqing and his followers Ruan Qishan, Zhang Bao, Cen Neng and Deng Suan; and the different branches of Yongchun Quan and their successors.

During the social turmoil in the late Qing Dynasty, Cai Li Fo Quan was introduced into Foshan. In the first year of the Xianfeng period (1851), Zhang Yan established the Hungsing Hall, which was deeply rooted at the bottom of the society to share the fate with the working people. In the various social transformations, its key members were at the forefront of innovations and played important roles in workers' and peasants' movements of anti-feudalism and anti-suppression. Subsequently, it was suppressed by the authorities and was out of sight for a whole decade since 1927. Many of its practitioners went to establish martial arts gymnasiums in Hong Kong and overseas.

In the late 1930s, Hungsing Hall was revived in the form of a sports association. Though still restricted in the political context, it managed to survive and thrive. Many of its disciples beat foreign boxers and made their name at home and abroad.

Nan Jia Quan emerged in Foshan in the late Qing Dynasty and the early Republic of China, with Liang Xisu as the great master. He was so low-profile and unobtrusive that the martial arts circle only heard of his name but not the type or origin of his martial arts. With its rich content, Nan Jia Quan is another case of the southward development of martial arts from Central China. It has been carried on in Foshan for over a century.

In the early Republic of China, martial arts competitions were held in Guangdong to select talent to serve in the army. Lin Shirong of Hong Quan, Zhang Liquan of White Eyebrow Fist, and Lin Yaogui of Dragon Style Fist all once served as martial arts coaches in Li Fulin's army.

Zhou Long was also one of them. By integrating Hong Quan, Cai Jia Quan and Shaolin martial arts he had learned, he established Zhou Jia Quan. Together with his four younger brothers, they were known as the "Five Tigers of the Zhou Family". The brothers Zhou Biao and Zhou Hai once performed together with Huang Feihong and Lin Shirong at the founding ceremony of Guangdong Jingwu Sports Association. Zhou Jia Quan spread widely in Guangdong and Guangxi and had branches in Shunde and Nanhai of Foshan. Since the 1930s, it has spread overseas, with martial arts gymnasiums all over the world.

With the introduction of modern sports from the West, people of insight who practiced traditional martial arts sought innovation and development in the changing times. Jingwu Sports Association, which broke with the forms and activities of traditional martial arts organizations and eliminated their patriarchal or religious connotations, adopted brand new dissemination modes of modern sports organizations and schools to publicize martial arts. The Sports Association promoted the urbanization and internationalization of martial arts, created and manifested their various values and functions, thus becoming a pioneer and model to promote the modern transformation and development of martial arts.

In the 1920s and 1930s, Foshan Jingwu Sports Association, as one of the 42 branches of the national Jingwu Sports Association, ranked the top in Guangdong and even the whole country in the inheritance, school running and cultural promotion of martial arts. It is an important base for the southward spread of northern martial arts. It is this association that brought Mantis Fist, Eagle Claw Fist and Taiji Quan, which are still popular today, into Foshan.

二十世纪二三十年代，佛山精武会作为全国精武会42家分会之一，在武术传承、武术办学及武术文化弘扬方面走在广东乃至全国前列。佛山精武会是北拳南传的重要基地，至今仍流传的佛山螳螂拳、鹰爪拳、太极拳均由该组织引入和传播。

鹰爪拳
周家拳
螳螂拳
洪拳
蔡李佛拳
佛山精武体育会
咏春拳

六合八法拳
白眉拳
龙形拳
南家拳
太极拳

第二节　泽被当世

中华人民共和国成立后，佛山市政府对民间武术社团进行重新登记，统一管理。1952年，国家体委设置民族形式体育研究会，将武术列为推广项目。1953年，时任国家体委主任的贺龙对武术提出了“发掘、整理、提高、推广”的八字方针，这对长期流传于民间的传统武术的发展产生了巨大的影响。

在1957年首届全国射箭武术观摩大会前的层层选拔中，全国各省、市、县的武术前辈和精英各展所长。彭南、区荣钜、曾坤等武术名家在佛山市传统武术观摩赛中脱颖而出，获得资格参加广东省体委在广州二沙岛举办的全省竞赛，其中区荣钜因成绩优异成为全国观摩大会的183名成员之一，为佛山赢得了荣光。

1978年11月16日，党和国家领导人邓小平题词“太极拳好”，给民间传统武术的发展带来了新的生机，中国武术从此进入了一个蓬勃发展的时代。1979年1月，国家体委发出《关于发掘、整理武术遗产的通知》。同年5月在广西南宁举办了全国武术观摩交流大会，乘借这一东风，佛山再次掀起了传统武术的研习热潮。

“1983到1986年，佛山市连续4年共组织了7次全市武术比赛，赛事拳种有龙形拳、白眉拳、蔡李佛拳、洪拳、螳螂拳及鹰爪拳

2 Benefits to the Contemporary Society

After the founding of the People's Republic of China in 1949, the Foshan Municipal Government re-registered the folk martial arts associations and put them under unified management. In 1952, the State Sport Commission set up a research institute for ethnic sports which listed martial arts as a promotion project. In 1953, He Long, the then Director of the State Sport Commission, put forward the principle of "discovering, sorting out, improving and promoting" martial arts, which has had tremendous influences on the development of traditional folk martial arts.

In 1957 in the selections of competitors to take part in the First National Archery and Martial Arts Observation Meeting, martial arts seniors and elites from various provinces, cities and counties all took part to demonstrate their skills. Peng Nan, Ou Rongju and Zeng Kun all stood out in the Traditional Martial Arts Observation Competition of Foshan and won qualification to take part in the provincial competition held by Guangdong Provincial Sport Commission at Ersha Island in Guangzhou. Among them, Ou Rongju became one of the 183 members of the National Archery and Martial Arts Observation Meeting and won the honor for Foshan because of his outstanding achievements.

On November 16th, 1978, the late Chinese leader Deng Xiaoping, inscribed the words "Taiji Quan is good", which has brought new life to the development of traditional folk martial arts. Since then, Chinese martial arts have entered a booming era. In January 1979, the State Sport Commission issued the *Notice on Excavating and Sorting out Martial Arts Relics*. In May of the same year, a national martial arts observation meeting was held in Nanning, Guangxi. Taking this opportunity, a new wave to practice and study traditional martial arts was set off in Foshan.

"From 1983 to 1986, Foshan organized seven municipal martial arts competitions for four consecutive years, involving martial arts types such as Dragon Style Fist, White Eyebrow Fist, Cai Li Fo Quan, Hong Quan, Mantis Fist, and Eagle Claw Fist. Martial Arts items have been listed as official competitive ones at various sports meets of Foshan. In 1984, Fenjiang District Martial Arts Association was established" [1], which later developed into Foshan Martial Arts Association.

At the joint initiative of its senior members, such as Mai Dahua, Ou Rongju, Huang Yingxin and Zeng Kun, Foshan Jingwu Sports Association was resumed in 1986. Different from the organizational and management structure when it was founded in the 1920s, the resumed one is no longer a subordinate of the General Association in Shanghai or the Guangdong branch. Instead, it has become a horizontal unity of various martial arts types and a big martial arts family in Foshan.

Since the 1990s, folk martial arts organizations, associations and gymnasiums have surged. Martial arts sports are prevalent in communities, villages and townships in Foshan. Among them, Taiji Quan has been promoted most vigorously.

Foshan Hungsing Hall was resumed in 1998 in the context of the comprehensive restoration and popularization of martial arts sports in Foshan. In the past two decades, it has developed tremendously and become internationally renowned.

In 1998, Huang Feihong Lion Dancing and Martial Arts Gymnasium was founded at Luzhou Village, Xiqiao Town, Nanhai. Huang Feihong Memorial Hall, completed and opened to the public in 2001, comprehensively demonstrates the life stories and related cultural products of Huang Feihong. It has become an important window for cultural exchanges between Foshan and other parts of the world, as well as a holy place for martial arts lovers from all over the world to explore Foshan martial arts.

1 The Compilation Committee of Foshan Local Chronicles. *Foshan Chronicle*. Beijing: Local Chronicle Publishing House, 2011, p. 2440.

等，武术项目列入佛山市历届运动会的正式比赛项目。1984年，汾江区武术协会成立。”[1] 其后汾江武术协会逐步发展为佛山市武术协会。

在佛山精武体育会老会员麦大华、区荣钜、黄颖心、曾坤等人的联合发动下，1986年，佛山精武体育会复会。与20世纪20年代建会之初的组织管理架构不同，复会后的佛山精武会，已经不是从属于上海总会或广东分会的分支机构，而是成为佛山各个拳种的横向联合体，成为佛山武林人士的大家庭。

20世纪90年代后，民间武术组织和拳会、拳馆的建立如雨后春笋般兴盛而活跃，武术运动遍布佛山各社区、镇街和乡村，尤以太极拳运动的推广声势为大。

佛山鸿胜馆在佛山武术运动全面恢复和普及的背景下于1998年复会，20多年间的发展可谓势如破竹，蜚声国际。

1998年，黄飞鸿狮艺武术馆在南海西樵镇禄舟村落成。2001年建成开放的佛山黄飞鸿纪念馆，多角度、全方位地展示了黄飞鸿的生平事迹及相关文化产品，成为佛山对外文化交流的重要窗口，也成为世界各地武术爱好者探寻佛山武术的圣地。

2002年建立的佛山叶问堂和2012年在南海罗村建立的叶问纪念馆，让更多人了解咏春文化，也让更多人爱上了咏春拳。

佛山武术根基深厚、纷呈多姿，是佛山多元文化的重要组成

1 佛山市地方志编纂委员会：《佛山市志》，方志出版社2011年版，第2440页。

部分，“武术之城”的荣耀使佛山文化名城的名片闪耀着异样的光彩。我们相信，随着《佛山市体育事业发展“十三五”规划》的实施与完结，佛山成为国际功夫中心和世界功夫之城的美好愿景就在眼前。

Foshan Yip Man Hall established in 2002 and Yip Man Memorial Hall established at Luocun Village, Nanhai in 2012 have enabled more people to understand the Yongchun culture and to love Yongchun Quan.

The deep-rooted and diverse Foshan martial arts are an important component of Foshan's diverse culture. The honor of "the City of Martial Arts" has made this renowned cultural city shine even more brightly. It is believed that with the implementation and completion of the "Thirteenth Five-Year Plan" for Foshan's sports industry, the vision of Foshan as the International Kung Fu Center and World Kung Fu City is in sight.